Make Food Work

HOW TO TURN YOUR LOVE OF FOOD INTO A SUCCESSFUL CATERING BUSINESS

Jeanie Gruber

Table of Contents

PREFACE
About This Book

WHAT CAN YOU DO WITH FOOD,
WHAT CAN IT DO FOR YOU, AND
WHAT THIS BOOK IS ALL ABOUT.

. . . .

Twenty years ago, I was contemplating the idea of making food my work. I wanted to regularly put my time, energy, and brainpower into creating and crafting edible delights. I wanted to devote myself to food the same way that, as a mother, I devoted myself to my two sons. I wanted to stand by the stove for hours caramelizing onions. I wanted to gift people with meals that were well-presented and delicious. I wanted to throw parties where guests talked about the menu for days afterward.

I had a few ideas. I thought about a "Gumbo To Go" company. I would provide Bostonian customers with a real dark roux, the kind that could only be made by a true Southern Girl. But it seemed like I would get bored cooking the same thing every day. "The Cajun Cab" was another idea. Cooking a full Cajun menu promised more variety than just cooking gumbo, but it still felt limiting. At the time, I was falling in love with Northern African spices and Thai recipes, and I couldn't imagine investing myself in a food product that excluded these.

So what kind of undertaking would work? It would have to offer the freedom to explore the cuisines of different cultures. It would have to be something I could do on a limited basis, so that I could keep my day job and raise my children. It would have to be something that allowed me to cultivate relationships with clients. For me, the answer lay in catering parties and other events. In this type of business, I found a way to work with food that worked for me.

But catering is only one of many ways you can take your love of food and make a business out of it. Whether you have a food truck, a coffee shop, a baking operation, or an off-premise catering company like mine, you are the owner of a food business. The majority of the details that I will expound upon in this book are relevant to anyone interested in launching any food idea. I'll share tidbits of wisdom that will resonate with anyone who has struggled with the common discouragements and obstacles that face food entrepreneurs.

Clearly there are differences between various food businesses. If you intend to sell potato chips to a local Quickie Mart, you will face issues that I, as a caterer, have not. If you run a food truck, you'll have to learn about regulations that are beyond the scope of this book. But questions like "Should I keep my day job?" and "How should I price my food?" and "Will this even sell?"—these are issues that one confronts regardless of what type of food product they launch.

Thanks to new opportunities and technologies, potential food entrepreneurs are no longer limited by age, sex, culture, or socioeconomic status. Anyone with persistence, determination and passion can get a food business underway. Initial obstacles like finding funding or cooking space can be surmounted more quickly and easily than ever before.

Whether you dream of catering corporate luncheons or selling homemade jam over the internet, I hope that the following chapters will serve as a down-to-earth, realistic, and heartfelt guide and will coach you in launching your idea.

My friends and family know there is nothing I love more than helping an old friend or a brand new acquaintance launch his or her dream, and I have indeed helped many a person get his or her business off the ground. I hope to be of similar assistance to you. It will give me the greatest joy if the following chapters inspire and help you to take your love of food and turn it into your dream work. I am certain you can make food work for you.

All Best,

Miss Jeanie

RECIPE REQUIREMENT: Something to
Spices Things Up

Nothing ensures the taste of your protein entrée more than a "rub." I've been sold on the technique since the first time I tried this tenderloin recipe. Try other rubs on chicken, lamb or turkey. You'll be sold too!

Orange Herbed Beef Tenderloin

INGREDIENTS:
2 tablespoons rosemary leaves
2 tablespoons fresh thyme leaves
4 large garlic cloves
1 tablespoon grated orange peel
1 tablespoon coarse salt
1 teaspoon black pepper
½ teaspoon ground nutmeg
¼ teaspoon ground cloves

Mix all ingredients in a food processor (adding olive oil last) to make a paste.

Rub paste generously on beef.

Place beef in a glass casserole dish. Cover with foil or plastic wrap and let rest in the fridge for anywhere between 16 and 24 hrs.

Cook beef at 400° F for about 35 minutes, making sure it reaches food safe temperature (140° for beef).

Let it rest for 10 minutes. Slice and Serve.

Your tenderloin can stand alone or you can create a sauce to accompany it, such as a Fresh Orange, Horseradish, and Sour Cream Sauce.

CHAPTER ONE
The Miss Jeanies Story

AS A SELF-TAUGHT CATERER, I NEVER DREAMED I'D
HAVE A STORY TO TELL ABOUT FOOD, MUCH LESS
ABOUT RUNNING A CATERING COMPANY.

. . . .

My journey to catering did not follow a straightforward path. No one in my Louisiana family was connected to the food, cooking, or baking business. However, my mom threw some great birthday parties. My parents also hosted a monthly supper club where the ladies brought their *Ladies Home Journal* recipes to share with the group. When they began their bridge game, I'd rush into the kitchen and sample them all.

As far as my love of cooking as a child growing up? Well, it was pretty much non-existent. I liked the eating, but not the work. I did envy my sister Ellen though. She could sew, cook, and bake. The big joke was that *I* couldn't even wash the dishes well. My family teased that I always seemed to head to the bathroom with a "stomach ache" until I heard the faucet turn off in the kitchen. Needless to say, no one ever allowed me to stir a pot, much less create my own dish.

But still, there was delicious cooking around me in the South of the 1950s. Much of it was already coming to life through generations of women in the African American community—with a lot of soul and a lot of seasoning. I'll always remember Alite, the woman who baby sat my sister and I. I'd pester her as she cooked on our patio during hot, windless summer days. I'd watch her spend hours at a time making mouth-watering dishes like Crawfish Bisque: simmering the roux, mixing together a Cajun bread stuffing, filling crawfish tails. The smells of this world were irresistibly inspiring.

There was always an excitement about food down South, no matter where you ate. Our family only went out to eat on rare occasions, and so ordinary restaurants were sources of intrigue for me. There was Hopper's Drive-In, where burgers and curly fries were brought out to your car by bellhops dressed in fifties garb. There was the Piccadilly, with delicious southern fried chicken and shrimp. They drowned their green beans in pork fat and cooked them until they lost their color. I even loved the smell of the prepared foods at the local A&P grocery store. If I close my eyes, I can still get a whiff of the cornbread and the slow- roasting Andouille sausages.

I ventured into my first food-related job in my twenties, while living in St. Louis and pursuing a graduate degree in Social Work. I was desperate for money. I'd tried retail; it was boring. I secretly worried that maybe I didn't like to work. But that fear vanished when the Ground Round hired me as a waitress and hostess. I loved going to work, talking to customers, and dealing with grumpy chefs. I relished counting my tips after a long day's work, even if they only amounted to change in my pocket. And I never minded the clean-up: sweeping peanuts and popcorn off the floor at closing time, breaking down the "outside of the house," readying the stage for the next day's drama.

After graduation, I moved to Atlanta and got a job at a one-of-a-kind restaurant called Aunt Charley's, where they turned out new and unusual menu items daily. I grew more and more curious about food, and I began to try my own hand at cooking. I eventually felt bold enough to talk Aunt Charley's owner into serving one of my recipes, "Broccoli Gruber," as the soup of the day. Although the era of "Broccoli Gruber" came to an end when I found work in the psychotherapy field, I still felt a pang of nostalgia every time I drove by good ole Aunt Charley's.

I continued working in psychotherapy after moving north to Cambridge, Massachusetts. I was deeply involved in my therapy career, and I loved it. However, I needed a way to satisfy my love of food. Luckily, it was the early 80s, and the culinary world was exploding around me. I discovered dark roast coffee and croissants filled with unusual fillings. There were pastas lightly doused with new sauces such as basil mint pesto. Fresh new greens framed delicate salads. My neighborhood, Harvard Square, came alive with all kinds of ethnic restaurants and cafés. Every walk through this epicenter of multiculturalism was an introduction to tastes and smells I'd never known before.

Back in my own kitchen, I started hosting parties and having people over to dinner. I found myself searching for reasons to have a party. My children gave me an excuse to labor over out-of-the-box birthday parties. My elder son's obsession with Popeye inspired his third birthday party: appetizers in spinach cans, Olive Oly's love potion as a beverage, a Pin-the-Tail on Popeye game. I did some great adult parties, too, like the Black Heart party that I staged for friends one Valentine's Day. I used black tulle and dark cloths in lieu of the typical red-white-and-pink palette. Romantic Blues played in the background while I served rich white and dark chocolates on black heart-shaped plates.

Still, I was no cook—but I wanted to become one. So I enrolled in an adult education cooking class. It was then that I fell in love with the magic of food production. My instructor was a charismatic, young woman who owned a local nouvelle cuisine restaurant. Her passion for African spices was palpable, as was the love with which she carefully peeled and diced garlic: she caressed it like a newborn. As I witnessed the transformation of raw ingredients into delicious cooked

So maybe my guests weren't always as into it as I was.

I still wouldnt let any excuse for a party pass me by.

items, I was enthralled by the beauty of it all. I knew then that cooking would be a key component of my life from then on. I began to read every food magazine and cookbook I could get my hands on and seize any opportunity to visit a new restaurant and sample new tastes. I was hooked.

Yet, still, the word "catering" never crossed my mind. I didn't know anyone who catered. And, well, I was a psychotherapist.

But then two friends asked me to cater parties they were throwing—one a fortieth birthday party, the other a library association get-together. I looked at both of them in disbelief, but I agreed. Looking back, I'm still shocked that I mustered the courage to accept those jobs, given that I'm not typically a risk-taker. But my enchantment with food, and my interest in developing artistic ways to serve it, were apparently forceful enough to catapult me way out of my culinary comfort zone. What could it hurt? I had my day job to fall back on.

I managed not to embarrass myself on either occasion, and soon I had another job proposition: a librarian who had been at the library meeting wanted me to cater a breakfast party. Despite the relative success of those first two jobs, I felt like a "fake," but I met with her anyway. We came up with the idea for a menu of breakfast foods featured in popular children's books. Our main entrée, Green Eggs and Ham, was accompanied by fruit-filled pancakes inspired by *James and the Giant Peach* and *Blueberries for Sal* (We desperately wanted to incorporate *Cloudy with a Chance of Meatballs*, but couldn't quite work it into a breakfast meeting). Several librarians who attended the breakfast requested my services, and before long I was catering library events around the city.

I went full speed ahead with catering although I considered it a hobby, not a business. Reality set in quickly, however: the logistics, the juggling of responsibilities, the long, hard hours. I lived in a whirlwind of activity. I would get up at four or five AM, cook for several hours, clean up the kitchen, get the kids ready for school, and run out the door. After spending the workday seeing my psychotherapy clients, I'd pick up the kids, cook for my family, and help with homework. Somehow, I'd get everyone to bed, and then I'd excitedly return to preparing food. A day was not complete unless I fell into bed, exhausted, practically cutting veggies and stirring soups in my sleep. I think I lived on adrenaline for years.

As I became more serious about catering, I speculated that I might need additional training, so I looked around Boston to see what was available. Although several esteemed cooking schools in town all offered a workshop or two devoted to catering, there was nothing beyond that, not even one course that went beyon the basics. I turned to books on the subject, but could find only one: *Catering Like a Pro*. I read it cover to cover. A little idealistic in tone, it lacked the down and dirty information I sought. I still had the feeling of being on my own, hoping I knew well enough what I was doing to avoid any really bad disasters. I wished for the chance to take a comprehensive training course about the practical aspects of running a small catering business. Even a mentor would have been a welcome relief.

Two years into catering parties I finally decided to give what I was doing a name: Southern Comfort Catering Company. A dear friend of mine surprised me with an impressionistic drawing of myself painted on a tray she'd picked up at a yard sale. This illustration became the inspiration for the company logo, which I printed on white linen business cards and stationery. My catering company felt official, but I still kept my day job as a psychotherapist I was content with catering as a part-time venture. Eventually I rechristened my company Miss Jeanies. We had one job per weekend, occasionally two. With all the other responsibilities I had, that was the maximum I could handle.

About five years into it, I began to reconsider expanding Miss Jeanies. I was receiving second and third generations of referrals, and I realized that I was in business for the long haul. With my elder son, Ben, graduating from high school and my younger son, Jake, finishing middle school, I had more flexibility with my time. With my husband's encouragement, I took the plunge and decided to open up my own commissary. When I happened upon a "For Rent" sign displayed prominently in the window of my fantasy building, a small bungalow with a

> ## I had always dreamed of opening a catering school one day.
>
> This was part of what enticed me about the space that became my first commissary: I knew that if and when I realized that dream, this site would be the perfect spot in which to do it.

front yard and pretty white fence located on a busy commercial street, it felt like fate. Within a few days, I viewed the space, met the landlord and his wife, and sealed the deal. Fortunately, the landlord's flexibility allowed me to put a commercial kitchen in the basement while using the first floor for offices and client meetings. I was on my way!

Now don't get me wrong: this was not done without fear, doubt, and anxiety. The risk of expanding almost overwhelmed me. I'd heard horrible stories about the difficulties associated with opening commercial kitchens: the health regulations, the inconsistent rules of dif-

PLEASANT STREET
COMMISSARY

ferent agencies, the challenges of finding and purchasing commercial equipment. I knew next to nothing about getting this stage of my catering business off the ground. All I did know was that I wanted it more than anything, and I was willing to work my hardest to make it a successful venture. Luckily, the process turned out to be far less stressful than I had anticipated, and in April of 2002, my staff and I celebrated the grand opening of Miss Jeanies' official catering establishment.

Life has its way of challenging you sometimes. Within days after the grand opening, I finally admitted to feeling more tired than usual. Concerned about my health, I made myself slow down and get a blood test. The unthinkable happened the following day. My doctor called to say I had to go immediately to Beth Israel Medical Center; doctors there confirmed that I had AML, a life-threatening form of leukemia. The next day, I was put on a chemotherapy regimen. While reeling from the sudden crisis, I realized that Miss Jeanies was catering a Bat Mitzvah celebration for 125 people—in two days.

Resolved to pull off the event, I told my nurses and doctors that I needed to meet with my staff. Of course, the hospital crew strongly objected. Finally I begged a doctor who had known me as a friend prior to my illness to advocate for me. I will never forget the words he told my oncologist: "Let her roll." And, with that command, the nurses brought a conference table and chairs into my hospital room. We followed through on the Bat Mitzvah, which turned out to be a success. For four long weeks we ran Miss Jeanies from the Beth Israel Oncology unit. We didn't cancel a single event. I am forever grateful to my loyal, gracious, and hardworking team. They kept Miss Jeanies alive, giving me the time, hope, and support to heal, which indeed I did. Miss Jeanies continues to thrive today, more than a decade after my leukemia was cured.

> When being treated for cancer, my concern with completing Miss Jeanies' jobs kept me sane. I diverted my stress over my illness to something under my control: keeping my company and reputation intact.

For years I have imagined that sharing my experience with Miss Jeanies could encourage others to turn their love of food and parties into a business. I know that it can be done with a lot of passion, organization, and motivation and without a lot of money.

CHAPTER TWO
Do You Have What It Takes to Be a Caterer?

IN THIS CHAPTER, YOU'LL LEARN WHAT
YOU NEED TO BE A SUCCESSFUL CATERER—
AND WHAT YOU DO NOT NEED.

In film and literature, people often wait tables or work in coffeehouses just to pay the rent. They have aspirations of being actors or writers or rock stars, and their day job is simply a way to stay afloat while pursuing their dream. But for others, working with food *is* the dream. They consider eating to be a near-spiritual experience. They see beauty in the raw products—the crisp veggies, aromatic spices, and fresh meats. They're in awe of the way a pinch of this or a dash of that can dramatically change a product.

For others still, the attraction is less about food itself and more about the opportunity to use skills like attention to detail, problem-solving, and perseverance. They get fulfillment from exercising such abilities. Another part of the attraction is that working with food provides an opportunity to create something, to start with pieces and finish with a whole. People also love food work because it's hard work. There's a reason why many hiring managers delight at seeing food service experience on a resume: succeeding in the food business means you're no slacker.

If you're wondering whether you have what it takes to be a caterer, or to run any other food business, remember this: certain skills can always be taught. Your success depends not on whether you can recreate the entrees served in a 5-star restaurant, but on the personal characteristics that we'll go over in this chapter. Read on and you'll see that you may very well have everything you need.

WHAT IT TAKES TO BE A SUCCESSFUL CATERER

You Need Stamina, Drive, and A Strong Work Ethic

To be a successful caterer, you need to have an extraordinary work ethic. You must like to work for the sake of working. If you don't relish hard labor, you will not be happy owning a small catering company, no matter how much you adore food. You need to be able to endure long arduous hours and plenty of unglamorous work. You need a willingness to work as hard as it takes to produce the best possible product each and every time.

As for stamina, you need to be prepared to hang in for the long haul, physically, spiritually, and emotionally, no matter the conditions. You need the physical strength to be able to work on your feet, move around non-stop, lift and carry items for long stretches of time. Even after all these years, there are times when I put in a 17-hour day!

In terms of spiritual and emotional stamina, you need to remain driven at all times, even when you're exhausted and ready to give up. Combined with your passion, your personal drive will propel you forward again and again, enabling you to produce a party that delights the client and brings you rave reviews, furthering your business.

You Need to Love Serving and Giving Food to Others

You need to have a love of giving to others through food. You may be an outstanding cook, but if you do not enjoy sharing your food with others, you will not enjoy the catering business for long. Even though catering is a business, when you share food that you've created, you are sharing something very personal.

Catering is definitely a service business. While there are times that, as the owner of your business, you may be treated as a "celebrity," you can just as quickly be perceived as a "servant." You need to be able to accept such changes in status. At every job, you are there to serve your client's needs, not your own. If you are catering your best friend's party, your best friend becomes your boss for the day: your duty is to serve her and make sure her needs are met, regardless of your personal relationship.

You Need to Excel at Handling Stressful Situations

You must have a quiet confidence that you can handle just about anything thrown your way. No matter how organized you are, there will always be at least one unanticipated situation that arises at any given job. Your success relies on your ability to greet such spur-of-the-moment challenges head on and successfully work through them.

You need to stay calm at all times. Forget all the shows on television featuring hollering chefs. Functionality among my staff decreases when I verbalize my stress; they've told me this. But keeping calm takes more than watching what you say or how you say it. My staff knows that when the blood vessels in my cheeks get a little redder, it's time for them to pick up the pace. In order to really keep your distress from being palpable, you need to cultivate an awareness of the vibe you give off through body language and other non-verbal cues.

Ideas for....

Keeping Calm

When I went into the catering business, I wasn't sure how well I would cope under this new breed of stress. I knew I wasn't afraid of hard work, but I didn't know if I was an on-the-spot problem solver. I knew that I had a pretty calm demeanor, but could I trust my inner strength to hold together hour after hour?

When things would get really tense on jobs, I often found myself thinking, "What are the worse things that can happen?" I used to answer with a spiral of catastrophic thinking: the soup gets burnt by mistake, the client becomes furious, she never hires us again, she tells her friends that we're inept, the referrals stop. But I've learned to flip my thoughts to "life is short, let it go." This inner dialogue allows me to calm down and generate the brain power necessary to solve the problems at hand.

You Need Good People Skills

You need to be able to work well with all types of clients and staff. Do you need to be a total extrovert? No, but your personality must convey sincerity, honesty, a real passion for your product, and a true respect for your staff, your client, and their events.

I do think it is critically important to be a good listener. You need to really hear what the client wants. I've found that most clients actually have a vision for their parties whether they know it or not. By truly listening to your client, you'll be able to help them conceptualize their vision. You can then impress your client by sharing how you can make that vision happen.

As a caterer, you form a relationship with your client—sometimes during the period that you work together, sometimes afterwards. You learn a lot about your client, their family, their personal likes and dislikes, and how they do things. You are brought into their personal life in a unique and special way. **The client-caterer relationship can**

and should be somewhat one-sided: it always focused on the client's needs, not the caterer's. It is certainly acceptable to share some of yourself, but my experience has been "less is best." Your client is always your boss. Once the party is over, there can be an abrupt cut-off in the relationship, which can feel strange. You will need to accept this as a reality of a catering business relationship.

As you become more experienced in the catering business, you will develop an intuitive sense of what will make a really successful event. You'll know when a client insists on something that just won't work or when they turn down something that's key to the success of the event. It is important to reign in your strong opinions and speak respectfully to the client, gently guiding them toward your perspective. If you share your thoughts and opinions too quickly or strongly, you may lose the job. On the other hand, if you do not share enough of your experience, you may be perceived as incompetent. **It takes savvy, self-control, and confidence to maintain balance with a client.** Having an open mind is part of the beauty of it all. When I put effort into understanding a client's perspective, despite any initial reluctance and concern about their vision, I will eventually be able to get into the flow, or "dance," with the client. And when that dance begins, and I start to feel the music, magic happens.

You Need An Entrepreneurial Spirit

You need to have an entrepreneurial spirit and a desire to work for yourself. You need the ability to manage your time well while working long, odd hours. If you like getting a steady paycheck from a nine to five job, then the catering profession is not for you. In all my years of catering, I've rarely had an eight-hour work day. Frequently my work hours are opposite those of the rest of the world. There may be weeks at a time when you work all day every day, and there may be weeks or even months at a time when business is slow. You will need to learn what can be accomplished during the slow times, when there are no events on the horizon, and you will need to get these things done.

If you like the idea of **having independence, constructing your own schedule, and creating your own rules and discipline**, then starting your own catering business may be right for you. But remember that the only boss you will have, besides yourself, is your client. There will be no one above you. To succeed at being your own boss, you must constantly guide, inspire, and motivate yourself. Rather than looking for the easiest way to do things, you need to seek out the best ways to do them and dedicate yourself to getting them done, no matter what it takes.

You must enjoy change, rather than wanting things to stay static.

Change and flexibility lie at the core of running a successful catering business. A good entrepreneur is always sniffing out opportunities, ways to improve and grow.

It's also important to point out that in addition to loving independence, catering entrepreneurs need to enjoy working on a team. Ideally, your team will work well together, be efficient and courteous, and will care about the product as much as you do. At Miss Jeanies, there is nothing like the "purr" of our team when we are in sync on a job. And, it shows—the client sees it, and I see it. The end result? A well-run, efficiently executed, and rewarding event that everyone—client, guests, staff, and you, the owner of the business—enjoy.

IS THERE BREAD TO BE MADE?

You can make money from the first day you sell your product, your idea. **You just have to be sure that the amount of money you are selling your product for is more than what you spent on the raw ingredients.** It's that simple. For example, a local convenience store has agreed to sell your secret special lentil soup to their customers. They have ordered 20 pots of soup a week:

INVEST:	SELL:	PROFIT:
Invest $100 and buy the raw ingredients needed for 20 pots of your soup.	Sell soup for $20 a pot; if you sell all 20 pots, weekly sales will total $400.	Profit $15 per pot, or $300 a week ... keep on going and watch it add up!

This is truly the simple basis of the dollars and cents of a catering business. Think about it. Once you've received money for your food products, your passion is no longer a hobby, but a profession! In creating menus, you will add more items, but as long as each time you make certain to sell it for more than your costs to produce it, you make money.

UNLESS YOU OVER-SPEND ON INGREDIENTS, YOU ARE GOING TO MAKE MONEY.

WHAT **ISN'T** NEEDED TO BE A SUCCESSFUL CATERER

You Don't Need A Lot Of Start-Up Cash

If you want to start by trying out a few products or a few meals, you will need very little start-up money. It is totally acceptable to ask for a deposit from a client to cover all your purchases; in fact, this is the industry norm. At the most basic level, you will need zero start-up money. This is why catering is one of the easiest businesses to try out. If you do continue with catering, it will take some start up cash to grow and expand your business. There will be additional food, décor, staff, insurance, equipment, and possibly even commercial kitchen costs if you go this route. We'll talk more about financing opportunities in Chapter 13.

You Don't Need A College Degree, Culinary Education, or Other Specialized Training

You do not have to have a college education nor have gone to a culinary school. Does it help? Sure, in the same way that all life experiences, training, and education can enhance anything you do. However, I believe that formal training in the culinary field does not guarantee a higher income or greater success or the ability to be a better cook. I have worked with both trained and untrained chefs in my years of catering. I have certainly noticed that some have developed more skills: they wield a knife quicker, make better cuts on food, or demonstrate an in-depth knowledge of certain food issues. These are all useful assets to a would-be caterer. Still, I have never felt that the formally trained chefs really made better cooks, managers, or business owners. In fact, sometimes their training and rigidity can hinder them when it comes to creativity, learning, and functionality. In reality, sometimes self-taught chefs and managers can be more open to facing challenges and to using flexible problem solving. They haven't had as many shoulds and musts drilled into them.

> Many owners of small catering companies begin as food lovers driven by an entrepreneurial spirit, not as professional chefs.

There are many ways to learn catering or cooking skills without attending culinary school. You might feel like you need to develop in certain areas before you start your business. Alternatively, you might get five years into your catering career before you think "I'm pretty darn good at most of what I do, but I could use some guidance in this particular area."

The easiest way to get a crash course in catering? Work for a catering company! Who would've thunk. Working for a catering company, you can quickly learn the ropes about how the entire process is carried out, from the first meeting with a client to the last goodbye at the end of the event. An evening or two of washing dishes at a 150-guest banquet can really give you insight into the inner workings of a catering company. Prepping and searing 300 chicken breasts can be a challenging but educational experience. There's nothing like being thrown right into the deep end to help you decide whether you really want to work as a caterer.

Technology is another avenue for building your expertise. You can scope out food-related websites, watch programs on channels such as The Food Network or HGTV, and even stream free video lectures given by celebrity chefs or famed universities. *Science and Cooking*, for example, is a lecture series offered by Harvard University and streamed online. Past lectures have included "The Science of Paella" and "Explorations of Chocolate." In-person adult education classes are another relatively affordable route for expanding your knowledge. In particular, a food safety course is a good investment (If by chance you live in New York, you're in luck! The New York City Department of Health offers their food safety class for free.)

Tales from Miss Jeanie

As you know, I taught myself the catering business. I would have loved to pick up a book or attend a course introducing me to the How To's of catering. But when I started out, there was not even one adult education class about the field. There was only one formal, and rather boring, textbook on the topic. Had I had access to more relevant information, I would have encountered fewer bumps in the road. As it was, **I often felt like I was flying blind, trying to develop a business with no information or guidance.** Although I came to see every mistake as a learning opportunity, that doesn't mean that I didn't need the help.

Becoming a self-taught caterer is much easier now than it was 15 years ago. You have more resources at your disposal than I did, thanks to an explosion of technology. If these technologies suit your learning style, then put them to your advantage!

You Don't Need Prior Business Experience

You don't need a business background to go into the catering field. You will, however, need to know how to do the following:

+ manage finances using basic math
+ write and express your ideas in a coherent, organized way
+ understand basic business concepts such as costs and profits
+ create systems of organization for clients' records
+ effectively communicate with clients, vendors, and staff
+ negotiate budgets
+ manage staff
+ maintain efficiency

You will need an accounting/bookkeeping method such as Quick-Books. I may have started out with handwritten bookkeeping, but now I find that technology makes my life a whole lot easier!

From the beginning, you will need to create a system of organiztion to contain the myriad of details from each client and event. Create separate files for each client—their likes and dislikes, their theme, décor, menus, preferences, etc. You can also use these files to help develop events for new clients, relying on your existing experience and information to help pave the way to success.

You will need to value efficiency. Hard work and labor will be a major part of your business, labor takes time, and time is money. As your business grows, you will get a sense for when to take short cuts and when not to. Your goal is to discover how to be as efficient and productive as possible. For example,. You may find that you're able to complete certain steps of a recipe, such as mixing together the dry ingredients for a bread, far in advance, thus reducing the work that needs to be at the last minute. You must also be able to change your ways of doing things, if necessary. For example, you may start out peeling your fruit on the day on the job, but eventually determine that this is too rushed. So you peel your fruit the day before the job, and wrap it very carefully.

Although it is certainly important to have systems, procedures, organization, and high standards of operations, you can't be a control freak when managing your staff. Staff can, and do, make many mistakes and it is critically important to have control over your reactions, Your way or the highway will not keep staff around for long.

Now How Do I Get Started?

If you're now feeling assured and hopeful about the possibility of starting and running a catering company, then your next question is probably "How to begin?". To start the ball rolling, it's time to turn your passion up full volume. You need to hit the "just do it" button. With your passion, drive, and the information you will acquire from this book, you will indeed find the right time and place to begin!

CHAPTER THREE
What Kind of Catering Fits You?

IN THIS CHAPTER, YOU WILL LEARN ABOUT DIFFERENT CATERING MARKETS, HELPING YOU TO DECIDE WHAT TYPE OF CATERING BEST FITS YOU.

. . . .

In a moment we'll get into the really exciting "how to" of catering, but first let's step back for a moment and take a look at the various types of catering businesses.

Before I started Miss Jeanies, I'd heard about caterers, but never hired one myself. I pictured them as business owners who employed staff dressed in starched white shirts and black slacks, servicing wealthy guests in an obsequious manner. Catering, as I imagined it, was frankly not something that appealed to me and not something I thought would ever be part of my life.

I certainly never knew there were different kinds of catering, and in my first ten years of the business, I didn't even know that I was providing a specific type of catering, one that had an official name to boot! I was just creating parties for people and loving it more and more every time I did it. Then one day I picked up a lone book on catering and learned I was running a type a small business called a Full-Service Off-Premise Catering Company. Who knew?

Full-Service Off-Premise Caterers are not the only caterers in town. In this chapter you'll read about three other types of catering:

Food-Only Catering

Chef Du Jour Catering

On-Site Catering

Defining Catering

Back in the sixties, we began every classroom paper or speech with the Merriam-Webster definition of the topic at hand. Since I love sprinkling a little retro feeling into everything I do, I'll revisit the exercise. The Merriam-Webster Dictionary defines the verb "cater" as "to provide food and service for."

Now, let's go current and look at Wikipedia: "When most people refer to a 'caterer,' they are referring to an event caterer who serves food with waiting staff at dining tables or sets up a self-serve buffet. The food may be prepared on site, i.e., made completely at the event, or the caterer may choose to bring prepared food and put the finishing touches on once it arrives."

Full-Service Off-Premise Catering is what most people are referring to when they speak of catering. This is the sort of catering that I know best and the primary focus of this book. If your company provides Full-Service Off-Premise Catering, you will offer the food, staff, linens, and dinnerware. You will produce the majority of the food at one location, then transport all of this to the event site. You may even coordinate the bar, décor, and other aspects of the event (We'll talk about this in Chapter 8).

And while the information in the upcoming chapters is written from the perspective of a Full-Service Off-Premise Caterer, you'll still find it applicable should you decide to pursue one of the aforementioned other types of catering or another food business entirely. These might actually interest you more and be a better fit for your skills and personality—so let's take a look at them!

FOOD-ONLY CATERER

Food-Only Catering offers great potential for creativity, profit and satisfaction. It is also a more flexible and less encompassing way to break into the business.

In Food-Only Catering, either the caterer delivers the food to the party site or the client picks up the food from the caterer. This involves no staff, no rentals, no decor, and no bar. It is an easier form of owning a catering company, as there are far fewer details to coordinate and much less intensive client involvement.

To get started as a Food-Only Caterer, you might create one or two items you love cooking. Maybe your friends and family have raved about them—their taste, their presentation, how unique they are—and told you that you should sell them. The item can be a beloved muffin or a family lasagna with a special sauce—anything that is made with love and perfection. So, you take a chance and sell a few muffins to friends, then a few more, maybe different muffins, then scones, a cupcake, chocolate mousse. Word gets out. Then one day a friend wants to do a little "champagne and dessert party" featuring your desserts. She'll supply her own liquor and paper products, rent her glassware, and even buy the ice cream herself—but she'll pick up the desserts from you on the day of the party. There: you're the owner of a Food-Only Catering Company.

I've always though that a fun, profitable Food-Only Catering concept could be something like a "Fusion Picnic Company," where you serve a limited menu of spring rolls, Asian salads and slaws, Thai wraps, and spicy noodles. Package the food in creative take-out boxes, enclose fortune cookies, tie the chopsticks in colorful raffia, and target outdoor and indoor picnics. Wrap it all up nicely in one big bag for the client to pick up, or deliver to the site for a small fee. In this way, you have the joy of creating, cooking and designing food for an amazing event, without the additional responsibilities of service, staff, and party execution.

Working as a Food-Only Caterer can provide a great opportunity to simultaneously partner with an established company and promote your own brand. For example, a local sandwich shop, Subbie's, is renowned for its selection of gourmet meats, cheeses, and condiments, but uses store-bought loaf bread. You, meanwhile, are a baker looking to sell your desserts, but haven't quite figured out how to fund the operation. You approach Subbie's and make a proposal: if they invest in baking equipment, you'll make the fresh bread for their sandwiches, provided that they allow you to bake your desserts at their site. The desserts will be branded independently—"Subbie's featuring Miss J's Cookies"—and clients will be able to come into the shop and order just Miss J's products. The beauty of this approach is that you can have your own catering company and distinct brand without having to provide your own commercial kitchen.

CHEF DU JOUR CATERER

A Chef Du Jour Caterer is a Health Department-sanctioned business designed for caterers who don't own or rent a licensed commercial kitchen. All cooking is done at the party site, so the menu must be carefully planned. Food items need to be such that they can be prepped quickly and pulled together at the last minute. Salads, seared scallops, couscous, etc., would work splendidly in this situation.

Chef Du Jour Catering is a great way to try out your catering aptitude. It takes very little up-front capital, limited equipment, and it's a great opportunity to experience the challenge of creating exciting and highly-functional menus. As you develop competency and contacts, you'll simultaneously be improving your catering instincts. These skills and potential referrals will prove invaluable whether or not you eventually decide to open a Full-Service On-Site Catering company.

Chef Du Jour Catering is a natural first step in becoming known as a niche caterer for smaller events. Because many large catering companies are reluctant to accept small jobs, there's an opening in the market for someone looking to cater dinner or cocktail parties, birthday celebrations, intimate family occasions, and the like. If you add up several of these parties per weekend, you could generate revenue equal to one large event, with much less stress and overhead.

You may find Chef Du Jour Catering to be a satisfying scenario for turning your love for food into a profitable small business. It's a great way to keep your day job while running a catering company. You will have control over how quickly you grow the company and how far you choose to develop it.

A Chef du Jour Menu

arugula salad with strawberries and goat cheese

seared curried lime shrimp

pistachio pesto orzo

aspargus with blueberries

ON-SITE CATERER

This type of catering is offered in a stationary facility. There is no transporting food to a party; the party comes to you. On-Site Catering Companies reside on privately-owned properties. For example, in large cities synagogues will frequently give exclusive rights to all on-site events to one catering company. Sometimes old VFW halls or churches, looking for creative new ways to produce revenue, will allow you to work on their site.

On-Site Caterers are also found at restaurants that have separate spaces for events. The caterer could be an outside chef hired to promote and run parties at the restaurant, generating extra revenue. This is a great place to explore pairing your catering company with an existing restaurant to create fabulous events in an already established space. For example, Maize is a local restaurant popular with couples seeking candlelight and escargot. Its success with romantic dinners, however, has not aided Maize in establishing a brunch business. You could work with Maize to create "Miss Jeanies Southern-Style Brunch, presented by Maize." The Sunday morning menu would feature your biscuits, grits, and mimosas; Maize would provide the site, supplies, and the reputation.

Another opportunity for On-Site Catering is found in law firms and large corporations that allow private caterers to run their own businesses within the company's space. At one point, my husband worked at a Boston law firm that rented space to a chef. This profitable partnership brought the chef independence, a guaranteed client base, and an incredible opportunity for menu creativity—all while allowing him to maintain a "normal" lifestyle. The law firm, in turn, saw his food as a perk for staff. The meals provided an incentive to work through lunch, and with gourmet meals available at dinner too, it was easier for staff to stay late. The chef was also responsible for all the food associated with the firm's meetings and parties.

This type of catering is an intriguing opportunity for people interested in starting their own business without some of the demands of Full-Service Off-Premise Catering. As an On-Site Caterer, you're relieved of the burden of loading and transporting all you need for a job to the site (you also avoid the multiple runs back home or to the supermarket, as something will inevitably be missing). Another benefit is the certainty of the space in which you produce events and a familiarity with the environment. Repeating events in the same space can lead to near perfect efficiency, thus freeing up extra time and creative energy to work on designing events, refining menus, and strengthening client relations.

I think On-Site Catering is a fabulous business if you're not big on last minute surprises, and you flourish with the consistency of having control over your environment. As an On-Site Caterer you will get to continuously recreate atmospheres within the same space, while creating different and exciting menus.

ARE YOU A SOCIAL CATERER, CORPORATE CATERER, OR BOTH?

I've frequently been asked this question and didn't really know what to say. I assumed all catering was social. On occasion, I did a party for a corporate client, but I never understood that there was a distinction. I just thought catering was catering. But, as the majority of the parties I have catered over the years have been personal celebrations, Miss Jeanies is in fact a Social Catering Business.

Social Catering had historically been almost exclusively for significant life events. But, increasingly, people are hiring caterers for smaller and more informal occasions such as cocktail parties or boat rides... practically anything imaginable goes!

Social Catering relies heavily upon client relations. Due to the personal nature of these events, your client's emotions, values, and sentiments are of the utmost importance. Over the years, when I told my story of going from psychotherapy to catering, people invariably were quiet for a long time...then smiled, nodded their heads knowingly, and said something like "Oh yes, I can see how your skills would be needed."

Although it is a less intimate type of catering, Corporate Catering requires professionalism, creativity, and the ability to maintain client relations with grace. As a Corporate Caterer, you can provide services for events such as product launches, retirement parties, holiday celebrations, and staff appreciation lunches. These scenarios demand you to be highly coordinated in executing events. You need to be on top of selecting the right food for the event and be able to manage your timing well. Often, you will also need to create atmospheres in sync with the culture of a company.

Ironically, the handful of corporate catering events we have done at Miss Jeanies left me feeling a little empty inside. I asked myself, "What was the point?" Yes, I was thanked just as much, yet I felt that for all the love and energy I put into the job, the client didn't seem personally invested in the results in the same way as social catering clients. For me, the corporate catering events felt more like a job, rather than a gift of art and food. But, don't get me wrong, client relations are still very important. If a corporate client likes working with you, your chances of gaining repeat business is much higher than they are with social catering., because they never run out of occasions. In contrast, how often does one's father have a 60th birthday party?

Flavor to Your Liking

No matter which of these possibilities you pursue, you will find that the basics I share in this book will apply to any of the above scenarios. Keep in mind that these aren't scientific categories: the catering landscape is an ever-changing one, and the most successful business ventures are often born of blurred boundaries. It's useful to know about all your options. Over time, you'll find a situation that lets you maximize your joy in providing your food gifts.

CHAPTER FOUR
Launching Your Catering Business in Seven Steps

SEVEN SEAS, DWARVES, AND DEADLY SINS—
AND NOW, SEVEN STEPS TOWARD LAUNCHING
YOUR CATERING BUSINESS.

. . . .

You've now determined that you have enough of the characteristics necessary to be a successful caterer. You've learnt that there's money to be earned, and that a culinary education is not a requirement. You've also learnt that there's surely a type of catering that'll be a fit for you (remember, the material in this chapter and those that follow is relevant no matter which form your food business takes).

Now you'll begin adding detail to your vision. When I started my business, I loved this part of the process, and I think you will too. The work of this chapter will exercise your creativity in ways that may seem challenging. If you get stuck, remember:

- *This is supposed to be enjoyable*
- *None of your decisions are irreversible*
- *You can always ask for help*

This chapter is divided into seven steps, each of which concludes with a To Do List. The components that you begin building here will ultimately form the foundation of your business. Spoon out your passion, heat up your work ethic, mix in some basic logistics, and begin.

STEP 1: PIN DOWN YOUR VISION

The first step is to determine your niche, your speciality, your love...what you want to be known for. Do you wish you could shower the world with one particular product? Do you have a mental image of yourself working in a certain setting? What can you do that will get people to lick their lips, praise you, and ask for your business card?

Don't fret if you don't have a firm version yet: just begin to verbalize the ideas and images in your head. Get down all your ideas, even those that are contradictory.

When you imagine your Best-of-all-Possible-Worlds version of catering, remember that catering is far more than food, and food is far more than a combination of chemical compounds. Think beyond how your product will be cooked—how is it portioned, displayed, accompanied? Then think beyond what you serve and how you serve it. With Miss Jeanies, for example, part of our speciality is that we put as much effort into decor as food. Low-waste catering, in which the caterer uses biodegradable packaging and composts whenever possible, would be another example of a niche that involves more than what's on the menu.

Don't worry if your focus feels too narrow. Don't think "I'll never survive if I only cater picnics." There's a difference between getting focused and holding yourself back. Businesses expand organically. I know

a frozen yogurt shop that recently started serving its product atop Belgian Waffles. Waffles most likely weren't part of the owner's original vision, nor will they ever be his speciality. He found a way to expand his business by riffing on his star product—gourmet frozen yogurt—and you will too.

At this stage in the game, be careful about sharing your idea. You may confide in a friend, colleague, or relative, but keep in mind that you need excitement and encouragement. Now is not the time to turn to that certain person whom you rely on for a reality check. There will be a time and place for their straightforwardness, but for now, you'll want to talk to someone who'll respond thoughtfully and enthusiastically when you bounce ideas off them. It is helpful if this person has business experience, but it's not necessary. The most important thing is that they'll help further your vision of running a successful catering business.

to do 1

Begin to find your catering focus by making a detailed list of everything you wish you could do with regards to food. Record all your ideas, no matter how unrealistic.

Consider how "bonus factors" like décor or packaging play into your speciality.

Choose no more than three friends or family members to serve as your "Advisory Board."

STEP 2: GIVE YOUR COMPANY A NAME

The initial name of your company should simply be something that feels consistent with your image and passion. That said, you can always change it later. I began with Southern Comfort Catering Company, then changed to Miss Jeanies Catering, and finally, Miss Jeanies Catering & Events Co. The only downside of these changes was the cost of reprinting my stationery and business cards. On the upside, each name change re-energized me and the business. In fact, many marketing gurus advise that a company should "re-brand" every seven years in order to stay current.

The winning name—for the time being, at least—may hit you while you're sleeping or in the shower, but when it does hit, you'll know. When that name arrives, go straight to the internet. Since a website for your company is an absolute necessity, you may even finalize your name choice based on the availability of a domain name.

If your desired domain name—let's use theplaidblanket.com as a case study—is already taken, try a variation on it, like plaidblanket-catering.com. This prompts the question, is the actual name of your business The Plaid Blanket or Plaid Blanket Catering? The advantage of the former is that it is your first choice, while the advantage of the latter is that there's no discrepancy between your company name and your web address. Consider this: an event guest asks one of your staff, "Who's the caterer?" and the staff member responds "The Plaid Blanket." That guest will go home and type theplaidblanket.com into their browser. They may soon realize that they're on the wrong track, and they'll hopefully find you by Googling something like "catering plaid blanket Boston," but why make them go to that effort?

Purchase your URL right away. If you're not ready to launch your website, just register the domain name. You do not need to pay for website hosting if you site is not yet "live."

to do 2

Look around at catering company names—in local resources, on Google, in your neighborhood, and at events. Write down three to five names you are considering.

If you are having a hard time coming up with names, ask two of your most creative friends or colleagues for some suggestions. Frame the question carefully: "When you think of eating outside on a blanket, what's the first thing that comes to mind?" will yield better results than "What should I call my company?"

Visit www.godaddy.com to make sure that the domain name you want is available. If it isn't, consider revising your choice.

STEP 3: CLAIM YOUR NAME

The degree to which you make your new company's name official is really up to you. Some people do not feel right unless their business' name is recorded in some governmental database. If you fall into this category, you will need to register your name with your municipality (city or town) and/or your state.

I pay an annual fee to register Miss Jeanies Catering & Events Co. as a Doing Business As (abbreviated DBA or d/b/a). A DBA means that I, Jean Gruber, run a business under a "fictitious" name. Even if my business were called "Jean Gruber's Catering," the name would qualify as fictitious, because the business name differs from my legal name. States have individual laws with regards to if and how you must register a DBA. In some states, like Massachusetts, DBAs are registered with a town or city clerk; in others, like Montana, they're registered with the Secretary of State. To find out the requirements and procedures for your state, contact either your state or local business licensing board.

Because your primary business competition will be local, in some sense it doesn't matter if people outside your immediate area use the same name. If you're a Rhode Islander set on the name "The Plaid Blanket," but there's a business called "The Plaid Blanket" registered in Nebraska, you needn't worry that you'll be competing for clients (they may even be an actual blanket company!)

But as I mentioned in the previous section, the problem with sharing a name is that the other company has probably laid claim to the domain name, not to mention the twitter handle, Facebook link, etc.

to do 3

Contact your local Business Licensing Board or visit www.sba.org to find out about registering your new business name as a DBA. If you're ready to proceed, contact your municipal clerk or Secetary of State, depending on the state in which you're located.

STEP 4: CREATE A BUSINESS CARD AND LETTERHEAD

Now on to one of the greatest parts of the prepwork—creating your business card. There are many options available to you. You could print the cards at home, at a local shop, or online. The advantage of establishing a relationship with a printing company, whether online or local, is that they will be able to help you with future needs, from menus for clients to a decal for your vehicle. As a general rule, local printers provide higher quality products, while online printers have lower prices.

Both local and online companies offer templates that you can use to create your business card. On the FedEx Office website, for example, a search for the keyword "cooking" brings up over 20 card designs that would be suitable for a caterer, while Staples offers a specific category of "Food and Beverage" business cards.

If you want to go beyond the basics, your options are limitless. A custom logo is one way to take your card to the next level. Perhaps it will be a drawing of a picnic basket, or an

The Plaid Blanket

Full Service Caterer Specializing in Picnic-Style Celebrations, Outdoors or In

Meg Miller, Owner

145 Maple Street
Omaha, Nebraska

402-581-4892

meg@theplaidblanket.com
www.theplaidblanket.com

old photograph of your mother in her kitchen (just be careful, as photographs may not look good when scaled to fit on a business card. Using a photograph as a logo will also require that you do all your printing
on high-quality paper, which can get costly).

I would suggest only having 100 or so cards made at first, to allow
you to make revisions without having to throw out too many cards. A
small initial batch will also reduce your loss if you need to reprint due
to a mistake on the card, but you can almost certainly avoid this by
having a friend proofread your card to check that all necessary information is there and that there are no typos.

to do 4

Type up three versions of your business card and stationery. Show
these to your Advisory Board. Have them choose a favorite and
explain why they chose it.

Call three local print shops and check out three online printing
companies. Get quotes on setting up and printing a minimum run
of business cards.

Select your printer, then either drop off or email them your information. Get a mock up design and proof it for errors before you
approve the final print.

STEP 5: DEVELOP YOUR ELEVATOR SPEECH

Several years ago I attended an entrepreneur's meeting where
members practiced and presented their own "Elevator Speech." Just
what is an Elevator Speech? It's a quick, seemingly impromptu explanation of your company and what you do, and it will become your most
natural and effective marketing tool. Your Elevator Speech needs to
convince someone to use your services, whether that someone is a
friend or a stranger. When you're starting off as a caterer, your success at generating business will rely on your ability to talk about your
work easily and quickly.

I always felt more comfortable having an Elevator "Dialogue" than
simply a Speech. When I meet a stranger in a grocery store, conversation may begin naturally. We talk about the line being too long, how
the tomatoes look, and the covers of the magazines in front of us.
After a few minutes of chatting, I may steer the conversation toward

finding out their line of work. When they inevitably ask me what I do, I'll say "I own a catering company." That does the trick. They flood me with questions. What kinds of foods do you serve or cook? What sort of parties do you typically cater? For how many guests? Where?

Sometimes I may just ask them if they like to cook. This leads them into talking about beloved foods or favorite restaurants. Connections formed around food are as instant and solidifying as those formed by dog owners who meet and bond over their pups. And once I get someone to talk about food, it's easy to bring up Miss Jeanies.

This is my elevator dialogue. I enjoy it, the stranger seems to enjoy it, and I have essentially pitched Miss Jeanies to them. Once I hand over my business card, my work is done. Sometimes I ask for their contact information so that they can be added to my mailing list. By that point, we've established enough trust that they are usually quite receptive to exchanging information. I hope that someday when they need a caterer or a friend asks them if they know of one, they remember our conversation and Miss Jeanies.

Try it out. You can always begin by discussing food and cooking. These are great icebreakers. People from all cultures and places love to cook. Talking about food can be revealing—a way to share who you are through what you like to eat. People will often be impressed that you have had the courage to take steps toward turning your love of food into a profitable business... steps toward making food work!
It's okay to say that you are just developing your business. You don't have to oversell yourself. As long as your passion comes through and you seem steady and reliable, you don't need to sound like you're a catering expert. Even if you haven't worked your first official job, you can talk about a party you catered cost-free for a friend or family member.

It might be that the person in line behind you is looking for someone to cater their wedding, i.e. the most important day of their life, and they just aren't open to hiring a newbie. On the other hand, they may be eager to give a new caterer a chance for another event or party— even the brunch following the wedding.

Hold Fast & Let Yourself Grow

Everything is subject to change. The variables discussed in this chapter, like your company name, marketing materials, and menus, can and will evolve. As you move into the next part of the process, your vision will stay steady.

to do 5

Compose your own Elevator Speech. Where are you? Who are they? How do you lead into a conversation about food?

Recite your Elevator Speech to a close friend, then see if they can tell you what you're all about. This will help make certain that you're getting across the right information and emphasizing the key elements of your vision.

Make a habit of practicing your speech when you're on the clock. Can you get through it all at a red light? What about in the space of one TV commercial?

STEP 6: CREATE SAMPLE MENUS & A MARKETING PACKET

The purpose of your menu is to show your client the foods you enjoy cooking, the tastes you value, and the style of parties you create. I would suggest drawing up at least three menus to show your first client.

To start, make a list of everything you'd like to offer: appetizers, entrees, desserts, and beverages. Recall dishes you've seen served at church or synagogue parties, family reunions, children's birthday parties, dinner parties for friends. Use recipes you've collected over the years. Above all, think about what you cook best and what you enjoy cooking. Don't put something on your menu that you don't feel confident about creating (Instead, start a separate list for "Reach" dishes—recipes that you need to practice and/or refine before you can prepare them skillfully).

You can also collect menus from other caterers, in person or on-line, to use as a jump-start for ideas. I think it can be really helpful in the beginning of menu creation to see what other caterers are doing. You'll quickly discern what you like or don't like about the way their menu items are selected and presented.

Once you have a lengthy list of items, organize your menus according to the type of event: a breakfast/brunch, a cocktail party, a sit-down dinner for ten, etc. One way to begin is to visualize a party. Describe the look and design: what colors and materials will you use? Will you set up five courses of Tuscan cuisine on a dining room table covered in a crisp white cloth? Are the guests seated or mulling about? How many guests are there? What temperature is the food?

Always have someone on your advisory board check your menus for grammar and spelling mistakes. Remember, your menu is a key part of your image. A client once came to me after having met with one of the more high-brow catering companies in town. She was appalled at the typos on the materials he'd given her. She saw the caterer's poor grammar as an indication that he was careless and worried that he'd approach her event with similar sloppiness. A well-designed and well-presented menu will go far toward making you look good.

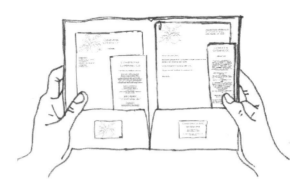

Once your menus are complete, compile a prototype of your Marketing Packet. If a potential client wants to see materials before scheduling a meeting, they're going to form their opinion of your business based on what you send them. To make a professional and thorough Marketing Packet, bulk it up a little. One possibility is to write up a short "About Us" pararaph that describes who you are and what sort of events you would like to cater. Another is to include images of your work, even if you just mock up some dishes specifically for photographing. Finalize your Marketing Packet by putting everything in a pocket folder. You can also visit the printer whom you befriended when designing your business card and ask about combining your materials in stapled booklets or folded brochures.

In this era of going paperless, it's a great idea to develop a digital version of your Marketing Packet. Make a full-page flyer that contains all the information contained on your business card. Compile the flyer, your menus, your About Us, and personal or stock photos into a PDF file that you can easily email to clients. This will save printing costs, help get your packet to clients instantly, and allow them to pass it on to an unlimited number of friends! If you don't have the computer skills to do this yourself, you can easily hire someone to do the project in an hour or two. You'll eventually recoup the cost of paying them by saving on printing and postage.

to do 6

Create at least three menus that characterize and express the feeling of your catering company

Write an About Us paragraph describing who you are & what you do.

Compile the menus, "About Us", business card, and any other materials you have into a Marketing Packet. Make sure to package it nicely.

Digitize your Marketing Packet so that you can email it to potential clients.

STEP 7: PRICING

Right now it is not important to worry about exact prices for your menus and events. At this point in the process, no new caterer would have a clue about pricing. Yet pricing is one of the most crucial elements of your business, and we will devote all of Chapter 7 to the topic. For now, just begin to think about the components of pricing: food costs, cooking costs, labor, décor, staffing, rentals, time.

It takes time to get pricing right, and in reality, there's no exact science to it. When you have real clients, you're going to determine your pricing based on the specifics of their job, rather than by referring to a one-size-fits-all pricing scheme.

Of all the variables discussed in this chapter, pricing is the most fluid. Take comfort in the fact that if your pricing structure doesn't work, you can keep changing it until you find one that fits...for now.

to do 7

Attempt to price out your three menus. Estimate your food costs, your shopping time, and your cooking time for each. Have fun with this exercise.

Start to notice how long food-related activities take. When you say "I'm running out for milk and eggs, be back in five," do you actually finish the errand in five minutes?

Explore what other caterers are charging. Try to find a company that caters the same sorts of food and parties you envision producing. See if your "guesstimated" prices are in the same ballpark as theirs.

Conclusion

Got through these seven steps? You're now dressed and ready to go. I consider a business name, website, stationery, business card, marketing packet, and sample menus to be the necessary "front of the house" fixtures to have as you meet your first client and launch your new catering company. Later we'll get to the "behind the scenes" fixtures, such as organizing your business, selecting vendors, and obtaining insurance. But first, let's see what the first meeting with your client is like!

CHAPTER FIVE
Meeting Your Client

YOUR FIRST MEETING IS A CHANCE TO LEARN WHAT YOUR CLIENTS WANT—AND SHOW THEM WHAT YOU HAVE TO OFFER.

. . . .

It's a plotline commonly found in the movies: a recently engaged couple quickly goes from over the moon to stressed and crazed. There are dates to coordinate, family members to deal with, and a thousand other details demanding attention. When you meet a client for the first time, you may be the fifth caterer they've talked to that week. It's easy to see why it would be important to make a good first impression in such a situation. But even when you're meeting a client who has already decided to hire you, or meeting with someone for whom you've worked in the past, the first meeting is still of critical importance. Think of the first meeting as an opportunity to make less work for yourself down the road: a thorough and informative meeting will give you an invaluable jumpstart on an event.

Preparation and Arrival

You don't have to wear a business suit or dress like a Wall Street executive. Wear something that will make a good first impression and, more importantly, will reflect your personal sense of style. Don't wear sneakers or casual shoes. You are the owner and CEO of your company, and you must convey maturity, responsibility, and reliability. Check that your hands and nails are clean and professional looking.

You absolutely must be on time for your meeting. Arriving late or worse, cancelling your first appointment can create a negative first impression. But if circumstances beyond your control are going to make you late, call the client immediately, explain that you've been delayed, and give an accurate estimate of your arrival time. Such courtesy goes

Starting from scratch ... or not?

The degree of communication you'll have with a client prior to your first meeting can vary greatly. Take the following two examples of client inquiries:

1) "Hi, my twentieth wedding anniversary is coming up and I just want to meet with a caterer to get some ideas. I was driving the other day and saw a van that said 'Miss Jennie's Catering,' and I wrote down the phone number."

2) "Hi, my wife and I are throwing a cocktail party for our twentieth anniversary. We want a Roaring Twenties theme. We're big fans of this speakeasy-style bar called Moonshiners, and we want to recreate that vibe. We got your name from our friend Natalie. We were guests at the birthday party that you catered for her, and my wife thought that your honey pork sliders were the best appetizer she'd ever tasted! I loved the quinoa puffs. We looked at your website and a lot of what we saw on the 'Nite Affair' menu would be perfect for us as we're hoping to stick to finger foods."

In the first scenario, the client has no idea what he wants. He hasn't even remembered your company's name accurately. He got your contact info off your van and cold-called you, which suggests that he hasn't chosen you out of interest in your specialty. In contrast, not only has the client from the second scenario already settled upon a theme and feel for their event, but they have expressed a particular interest in two of your products and a particular menu.

This chapter focuses what to do with clients who don't yet know exactly what they want. But if a client has already established in great detail what they're looking for, you'll want to tailor your marketing packet based on the information they've offered. With these cases, you've got to get a jump start on your proposal before the meeting. Read about Prohibition and the twenties on Wikipedia. Try to find photos of a speakeasy. You could even take a shot at composing a "working menu" that features the appetizers they like—quinoa puffs and honey pork sliders—with seven or eight additional suggestions.

far toward appeasing your client and establishing your reliability.

If pushing back the meeting is going to cut it too short, apologize profusely and suggest a rescheduled time. A delayed or cancelled meeting doesn't necessarily render your client relationship dead-on-arrival, but it does get the relationship off to a bad start. This can be hard to overcome, even if you've been highly recommended and/or already have a great track record. In the first year of owning a company, making unnecessary mistakes will cost you business.

Sometimes your client will be the one who runs late. Avoid having something on your schedule right after the meeting, so that if the client needs to push things back, you will still be able to spend enough time with them. And if the client asks you to reschedule, don't make them feel like they're inconveniencing you.

Make sure to bring a copy of your Marketing Packet to your first meeting. Be prepared to take notes. I find that clients appreciate it when you bring along some paper and a pen for them to write down their own notes. If you have a laptop or tablet with wireless internet, bring that as well. You don't have to pull it out initially. However, if the client says, "I want you to make my backyard look like a resort on the Greek coast," hopping online can help her demonstrate what she's envisioning.

Tips for ....

Meeting at Your Clients Home

Remember your purpose. It can be easy to forget your professional demeanor when you're sitting on a couch, party planning.

When you arrive, lightly compliment your client on something that strikes you as interesting or aesthetically pleasing. A person's home is always filled with items that are important to them and they will appreciate your attention to this.

If the client offers you coffee, it's okay to politely refuse. You want to communicate that you are there to focus on the event.

Your Meeting Begins

Get down to business relatively quickly. If your client has already given you some information via phone or e-mail, start by reviewing that. Going over the basics can be a great jumping-off point. Next I like to ask the client if they prefer to begin with my questions or theirs. Often they'll have questions that they're eager to get on the table.

If they wish for me to take the lead, I start by asking if they have a vision of the event. Do they have ideas about the menu, the décor, the schedule, or the general feel? If the client seems overwhelmed by all these questions, you can offer your ideas and agenda instead. Sometimes I will help move things along by describing a recent event I catered. Alternatively, I might describe some of our more popular menus, events, or themes. Even if a client shakes their head "no" at everything I recount, we make progress: understanding what a client *doesn't* like is a step toward understanding what they do.

Find A Hook

The goal of your first meeting should be to find "the hook:" something that will be the central focus of the food or event. Having an underlying theme ensures that you and your client stay focused and that the event will ultimately "make sense." By "theme" I don't necessarily mean Hawaiian Luau or Masked Ball. "Light and Fun" could be the hook; so could "texture" or "quiet" or "spreadables" or "Things Guests Have Never Eaten Before."

You will know the hook when you hit it. It's a wonderful moment: the client will get enthusiastic and noticeably energized. But don't worry if the hook proves elusive. If you reach the end of your conversation without having found it, then you can always say, "We've discussed some great ideas and I've gotten a good sense of what you like. Let me head back to my office, pull your ideas together and let them percolate.

Questions to help you ...

Find the Hook

What are your client's favorite foods? Family Recipes? Restaurants?

Have they attended parties that "wowed" them?

Is there one item they adore or always wanted to eat?

Any ideas from their travels?

Did they hear about an interesting food or theme on a cooking show or from a friend?

Is there an object that could serve as the focus of the menu or event presentation?

I'll get back to you in the next few days with a proposal." If it's been a stimulating, purposeful discussion, your client will be satisfied for the time being and will await your the proposal.

Address Special Requests

On occasion, a client may want the menu to include an item I've never cooked. When I was first starting out as a caterer, I probably responded overenthusiastically if a client requested that I create something difficult or unfamiliar. I didn't want the client to lose confidence in my abilities or think me inexperienced. Nowadays, I'm confident that I have sufficient culinary skills and research capacities to make things that are not my norm. I don't pretend to be an expert chef, but the difference is that I no longer think I need to be.

Determine the Schedule and Scenario of the Party

Another matter to discuss in your first meeting is the schedule of the event. It is important to understand what the client has in mind regarding the length of the event, the sequencing of food, the distinctiveness of courses, and more. It will be wise to discuss the pros and cons of different scenarios with them.

At events with both kids and adults, there will often be two schedules. The kids may have their main course while the adults are still on appetizers. Or maybe a DJ or MC will engage the kids in party games while the adults eat a plated first course.

Even at adult only events, scheduling can take on a dizzying number of variations. At a dance party, for example, does the client want an hour or two of serving food before dancing breaks out for the rest of night? Or should there be food available throughout the whole evening, with guests choosing to eat or dance as they please?

Questions to help you ...

Plan A Schedule

At what point during the event should the serving begin?

Are there separate schedules for kids and adults?

Should there be breaks between courses?

Should the bar stay open all evening?

Does the ambiance change or remain the same?

Explore The Décor or Design of The Event

Many caterers do not offer to take care of the décor and design for an event. But one thing that's unique about Miss Jeanies is that we try, whenever possible, to do not just the food and staffing, but the décor as well (check out Chapter 8 for more on this). This was part of my vision from the start.

Still, some jobs have no décor. For others, the client will do the decorations or hire a party planner. Sometimes I'll arrive at that first meeting to find that a party planner is already in the picture, and the major décor questions have already been decided.

By bringing up décor at the first meeting, you'll know off the bat if the client has hired an event planner, florist, or other relevant vendor. This lets you get a sense of division of labor for the whole event. If a client tells me they want 500 silverware sets wrapped in napkins, I need to know whether my staff is going to be responsible for assembling those. The budget I prepare will vary based on whether I need to have three staffers arrive a couple hours early to roll silverware, or whether an event planner will be doing that job.

Even when the client hasn't asked you to do the décor, the décor is part of your job. You are responsible for finding the ways of presenting your food that will best compliment the décor and ambiance of the event.

Linens and China

Another area to clarify at the first meeting is the client's preferences regarding linens and china. At some intimate events, the client will provide tablecloths, napkins, dishes, cutlery, and glassware. But most of the time, unless the client is planning to use paper plates and tablecloths, the caterer will need to rent china and linens from a party rental company. Most caterers charge a 10-20% service charge to rent linens for a client. Handling the linen rental and passing on the service charge can generate additional revenue for you.

Many clients, especially if they're working with a caterer for the first time, will need to understand how a caterer interacts with a rental companies. They will want a sense of cost, and will frequently ask for your advice in comparing costs of disposable versus cloth linens and paper products versus china. If you have noticed a pattern in preferences based on your work with different occasions and client groups, it could be useful to share your opinion. These decisions are ultimately personal, however. Some clients may never consider using paper linens, no matter how expensive the cloth ones may be. Others, depending on the situation, will consider using them to keep within a tight budget, and may prefer to spend their extra money in other areas of the event.

On that note, by this point in the meeting, you should be getting a sense of your client's taste. Even if you haven't been to their home, you've spent time together, heard the way they speak, and learned about their vision. Think of taste as more of an aesthetic sensibility, rather than something related to social status. For example, does the client strike you as a minimalist? Are they adventurous? Cautious? Do they seem out of their element when discussing parties or have they "studied up" on the subject?

The need to get a feel for a client's taste and values is one of the reasons why I suggest having our first meeting at their house. A client's home, coupled with their words, provide invaluable clues in helping you find the right menu and feel for their event.

Get The 411 On Key Contact People for the Event

As you begin to conclude your meeting, be sure to obtain any names, phone numbers, and email addresses that your client feels are important. I often find that a client will designate a spouse or friend to serve as the decision-maker during the event, and I make sure to get the contact information for that person. Having a designated contact person during the event means that the client can enjoy themselves while feeling confident that the staff has someone to consult when questions arise.

There are many other people who make an event happen. These could include:

+ DJ or Band
+ Master of Ceremonies (M.C.)
+ Event Designer
+ Bartender or Liquor Company
+ Rental Company
+ Function Hall Staff

A bonus of knowing whether these parties will be involved is that it helps you understand the magnitude of the event. You'll find such information to be helpful in Chapters 7 and 8, when you're figuring out how to price your job.

It is also important to set the stage for directly communicating with your client throughout the entire working relationship. Tell your client to contact you with questions or ideas during the period leading up to their event, even up to the last minute. Explain that you will call or email them back as soon as your schedule allows and reassure them that you will always remain hyper-focused on their event. If an urgent matter arises, they can let you know and you will call them back as soon as possible. If this should happen and you are unable to respond immediately, it is fine to have a senior staff member return the call and ease the client's fears with a quick response. Clear, open communication from the start will help maintain a client's confidence and trust in you.

> **Little Extras...**
>
> ## Find the Rhythm
>
> Whether a night-time event, a brunch or dinner party, it doesn't hurt to have music as a nice, inexpensive addition. It can always enhance the spirit and feel of any event.
>
> Would your client want music to serve as part of the background and décor, or would the aim of the music be to get people up and dancing? Whether using DJs, a band , or even a client's own digital playlist, there are several ways to bring a party to life with music.

Future Process

As you conclude your meeting with the client, outline your next steps. Tell them you will pull together a proposed menu based on what you have just discussed. Within the coming days, you'll establish the basic menu and gather estimates from all or any auxilliary vendors in order to send the client a proposed estimate for the event. Before your meeting ends, let your client know when they can expect your proposal, adding that you will call them should it take longer than anticipated. Now is also the time to explain that once the client has accepted your proposal, the two of you will either sign a contract or agree verbally to the terms of your business relationship. Finally, explain your deposit requirements, refund policies, and other business provisions. You can refer to Chapter 9 for guidance in how to establish these policies.

On Your Way Out

As you leave, be sure to enthusiastically share how much you have enjoyed meeting with the client and laying the groundwork for what will be a wonderful event. Always leave the door open for any questions or concerns you client may have about the event. Encourage them to keep you updated as the big date approaches. If your client hasn't fully committed to hiring you as of yet, be sure to emphasize how much you would like to work with them and how you hope your budget, menu, and ideas will
"hit the spot."

CHAPTER SIX
Building Your Menu

START A MENU FROM SCRATCH:
BE IMAGINATIVE, CREATIVE, AND PRACTICAL.
ENCOMPASS YOUR CLIENT'S VISION.

Relief. Excitement. Apprehension. Your first encounter with your client is over. After mine, I reviewed how my suggestions had been received, what I had learned about the client, and the ideas we had begun to formulate; all that stimulation made me desperate for a strong cup of coffee. I had told the client I would get the proposed menu and budget to her within a week, which seemed soon enough. Nowadays, if a client seems enthusiastic and ready to commit, I aim to get her the proposal even sooner. But regardless of whether you're putting a menu together in a week, a day, or a month, the components needed to craft a successful menu will be the same. In this chapter, we'll review those factors, which I've grouped into four rough categories:

1. Understand the Logistics of the Event Site

2. Start with the Overall Experience

3. Think About What Will Work

4. Think About What People Want

Now, get ready to go. You don't need a stable office yet, but remember the importance of keeping records as you work. Keep track of foods you consider but decided to omit and other ideas that were "wrong time, wrong place." Someday you'll be glad you have documentation of your catering business's history, process and progress.

ONE: LEARN THE LOGISTICS OF THE EVENT SITE

The first step of creating your menu is to visit the event site. Of course, if the event will be held at your client's home, and your client meeting was held there, then you have already had the opportunity to look over the kitchen and notice the "flow" of the home. Regardless of whether the site is a home or a public space, every event space bears unique properties that form challenging, yet exciting, elements to work around. The layout and capacity of the site will affect what you will feature on your menu—and what you charge. Without an understanding of the party site, you may create a logistically unrealistic menu that will cause you all kind of headaches, hardships and heartaches on the day of the job.

> The LAYOUT and CAPACITY of the site will affect what you will feature on your menu—and what you charge.

If the event is not being held at the client's home, you should schedule an appointment to visit the site (you can also try your luck at popping by for a quick peek). While there, evaluate whether the kitchen design is congruent with the demands of your potential menu. Think about these questions:

* How large is the kitchen? Is there adequate space to set up the job, produce the food, and sequence the menu?
* Is there a stove top and oven? How many?
* Are you allowed to grill or fry?
* Is there adequate refrigeration for storing cold items?
* Can the electrical wiring support your appliances?
* Will you be able to rotate dishes and flatware by washing as you go, or will all the dishwashing need to be done at the end of the event?

If your client is having a party at their home, you'll likely run into greater difficulties than you would when working in a commercial kitchen. The space will rarely be ideal, and often it'll be downright unreceptive to your vision. In such cases, get creative in making it work. At Miss Jeanies, we have made makeshift kitchens out of utility rooms and garages, plated courses on laundry machines, and created coolers by packing bathtubs with ice. Your client will appreciate your optimism and perseverance in transforming a seemingly unworkable space into a functioning party site.

Miss Jeanies' Wisdom:
EVENT SITE LOGISTICS

When a client asked me to cater a party at a local boat club, it was clear why she'd picked that spot. The newly-built facility was conveniently located with spectacular views of the Charles River; the huge open space on the second floor was perfect for a party. The only problem was that the building's developers hadn't given proper thought to how profitable it would be to rent the space out for events! As such, the building had just one teeny-tiny galley kitchen, with a single sink, no dishwasher, and practically zero counter-space. To make things more complicated, the menu was a complex one featuring separate dishes for kids and adults. But with a little brainstorming, I came up with a menu that could be heated onsite in convection ovens. I got the OK from the facility's management to set them up in a classroom off the main function space

On the night of the party, we warmed appetizers in our rented ovens, and began passing them to the happy crowd. We continued to warm appetizers and were beginning on the main courses when the electricity started to flicker. The onsite manager didn't have a clue where the electrical boxes were located or how we could reset the fuses that had apparently blown. The main course was still cold, and I began to fear that we were going to be forced to order takeout! The onsite manager suggested that we move the convection ovens to another room far down the hall. This meant relocating our entire operation! Staff had to walk past the guests with pans of uncooked chicken, acting like nothing was wrong. The ensuing panic hurt our coordination. I debated whether I should tell the client what was going on, and decided against it.

In the end, we got the food out and pulled off the event. There was even a positive outcome: the boat club, taking responsibility for what had occurred, investigated the location of all their wiring and drew up a map so that in the future, caterers and other service workers would know how to avoid overloading a particular grid. As for the client, she only had one negative thing to say: she wished we'd informed her of what was going wrong as it occurred instead of keeping her in the dark.

It wasn't long before I had the opportunity to cater at that boat club again. Thanks to my improved knowledge of the site's logistics, I felt comfortable taking the job. This time, we cooked the main course offsite to reduce the chance of overloading the electricity. I even had an "In Case of Emergency" menu planned. We've now done nearly a dozen events at this club, and while they're getting easier with time, I do charge the client a premium price due to the inconvenience of the site.

TWO: START WITH THE BIG PICTURE

The Gestalt

The concept of a gestalt—"an organized whole that is perceived as more than the sum of its parts"—is critical to menu planning. **A menu should be experienced as a unified whole, not a haphazard arrangement of foods.** Offer a collection of complementary flavors, textures, and colors served and presented in a way that makes sense and feels good to the client and guests. The overall impression of the event matters more than achieving a mathematical balance of food. If it makes sense to feature six savory appetizers and a single sweet one, then do so. Keep it in mind that balance doesn't necessarily mean equity.

Beginning, Middle, and End Experience

Every eating experience should have a beginning, a middle, and an end. The model that we're most familiar with is appetizer, main course, dessert, but there are many ways to maintain a beginning, middle, and end while varying from this standard structure. If you are creating a menu that is all *hor d'oeuvres*, for example, you can define a beginning, middle, and end by transitioning from simple foods to more complex ones, or from savory to sweet. You could also mark distinctions by having different courses served or presented differently.

> Ideas for....
>
> *Creative Coursing*
>
> Do as the Europeans do and serve the salad course after dinner.
>
> Open with something sweet, like Brie and fruit, then progress towards savory foods. Finish by returning to something sweet, like a classic, rich dessert.

The Wow Factor

You can create a fabulous party that will engage imaginations by adding a "wow factor" to your menu. Depending on the size of the party and nature of the event, there can be room for more than one wow factor. But, be careful about offering too many bravura moments. This can end up like a fireworks display—after a while everything starts to look alike, and the shimmer is lost. You don't want to try too hard. Instead, spread out the wows and keep them coming. Also, a wow need not be loud. Finally, don't neglect the other items on your menu: I firmly believe that every item should have its own presence and integrity, whether or not it serves as a "wow factor."

The Four Food Groups

For many people, a party serves as a welcome break from eating healthfully. Still, a menu often includes items from each of the four food groups: proteins, carbs, fruits, and vegetables. Sometimes, if a client chooses, you can purposefully create a more vegetable-laden menu or a more protein-heavy meal. I even had a client who adored fruit, bread and chocolate—not your traditional food groups—and requested that I focus on these items. Hers was a black tie affair, however, and keeping in mind that guests might not appreciate this limited menu at an evening event, I did include other buffet stations with proteins and carbs for balance. Still, the chocolate, fruit, and bread held center stage.

Food Aesthetics

You really don't have to worry about matching colors and textures of the food on your menu, nor about how often you repeat those colors and textures. Popular opinion is that a menu should be as varied as possible, but I don't think that's always necessary. If the items most suitable to the menu turn out to be brown and pale, there are design strategies to help them pop. Adding a simple garnish or placing a flower bud between a parsnip and a potato can turn a dish into eye candy. Furthermore, many crunchy tastes together can be exciting. And, repeating the same foods, such as cheeses in every item or tomatoes in every dish, can offer a comforting consistency. If the items are individually delicious and fit the gestalt, you can repeat them.

THREE: DO WHAT WILL WORK

Cook What You Do Best

As a new caterer, choose dishes to distinguish you from the other cooks in town and therefore help you establish your brand. But make sure you can do this with competency. Your hostess and guests will know if you've gone beyond your expertise, no matter how far you are stretching to be a sensation.

If you have an item that you think you do especially well, try to weave it into your menu. At Miss Jeanies, we found our fig quesadillas to be a hit. Everyone, no matter the event, would beg for our recipe. Whenever possible, I would put the quesadillas on the menu, sometimes just adding them in as an extra treat. The hostesses were delighted. So, if guests rave about a signature item, enjoy the accolades and give it as much play as possible.

Ability to Find Items

Locating hard-to-find items or seasonal ingredients can have a big impact on what you plan in your menu. There have been times that I read or heard about items that I felt would spark a menu, but I hadn't seen them in my local markets. Despite the wide assortment of multi-ethnic vendors in my city, I had to search for days, making endless calls, trying to track down the ingredients.

In order to address this challenge, especially if you live in a smaller community where your access to supplies may be limited, you may need to ask your local grocer to locate an item. With enough advanced notice, a grocer will take the time to locate items for you, especially if they sense that you may eventually become a steady wholesale customer (See Chapter 14 for more on this). Understandably, you may have to pay a little more if the grocer is only supplying you with a few custom items, but the satisfaction of finding a key item usually makes up for the added cost. A client appreciates this too!

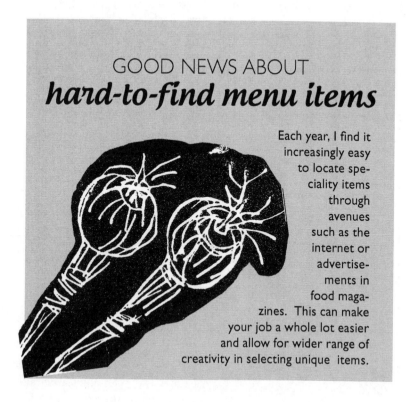

GOOD NEWS ABOUT
hard-to-find menu items

Each year, I find it increasingly easy to locate speciality items through avenues such as the internet or advertisements in food magazines. This can make your job a whole lot easier and allow for wider range of creativity in selecting unique items.

Seasonality

I've been surprised to find how many clients consider the seasonal aspect of their parties and want menus incorporating foods associated with the time of the year of their event. At certain times of the year, people just feel like eating certain kinds of food. Mini ice cream sandwiches will hit the spot at a 4th of July party, while hot chocolate with Oreo-flavored whipped cream will delight a company holiday gathering.

As a twist, you may find a beloved summertime regular can be an amazing treat during the long days of winter, reviving the hope for warmer days. Once, I had a client who wanted a summer BBQ for an event held in the icy days of January. To meet this request, I had to compromise the perfection of some of the ingredients: the corn in the corn salad wasn't as superb in January as it would have been in August, but with enough lime, cilantro and red onions, I made it work. However, a tomato/mozzarella/basil salad would not have worked: January tomatoes were just too tasteless to make a standout caprese.

Keep in mind that you may be planning a menu in October for an event that's not scheduled until June. I often have to remind myself that the delicious apples delighting my senses during fall will not stimulate the same sensations come the early summer months. If you're not sure when in the year an item will become available, ask the staff at your grocer. An internet search is another way to find lists of when specific seasonal fruits and vegetables become available in your region.

Food Quality

One of the most critical determinants of food quality is whether the items will reheat—remember that as a full-service *off-premise* caterer, you'll be doing the bulk of your cooking before the event, thus making items that reheat well particularly important to your menus. Some food just "dies" when not served piping hot—those will be the dishes you cook on the spot. **Determining what can be reheated and what needs to be cooked at the last minute is one of the hardest parts of catering** and continues to be a challenge over time, although I promise, you will begin to develop a expertise in this area.

Whenever you're working with a new recipe. I highly recommend that you make it ahead of time, put it away, take it out and see how it reheats. Note how long you cooked it and whether you needed to rebaste or reseason it. Figure out every step between taking the item from the refrigerator and serving it to your guests.

If your menu is loaded with many items that need to be reheated at one time *and* at the last minute, and you only have one stove, you will create a nightmare for yourself (Then again, remember when you visited the event site and checked out how many stoves were available? If there were quite a few, this may be the perfect opportunity to create a menu featuring those types of items). Be sure to have some items that can be reheated before "showtime," and can sit for a while without hurting their quality. You can just pop them back into the oven for one minute immediately before your serve them. Also, plan some items that can be reheated on the stove top burners (as opposed to in an oven), or items that will be cooked on the stove top for the first time. Add in some items that are delicious when served cold or room temperature or ones that can be prepped the day of the party and kept in the refrigerator to be brought out when you need them. Even if you are a cook that doesn't like a lot of sauces, have some toppings available to help enrich an item should you overcook it when reheating.

Outsourcing Items

When it comes to outsourcing, the bottom line is: don't fight it. If there's something you really want to have on a menu but you can't do it on your own, then outsource. Initially I would not have dreamed of serving anything cooked by others, imagining that the "catering police" would catch me within minutes of the onset of the party. But as it stands now, outsourcing is considered acceptable in the industry. On occasion, I will buy cookies or pastries from a local bakery. And I definitely find it acceptable to buy fresh breads on the day of the event, especially when the client doesn't expect me to produce them myself.

Looking back, it was sushi that forced my hand on this. I had become quite busy, and as much as I wanted to become proficient in constructing sushi,  I just didn't have the time. Instead, I researched the local place with a reputation for producing the absolute freshest sushi and ordered it to be made at the last possible minute. I was pleased to see that this worked out. Such experiences have increased my comfort with outsourcing items. There are just some things that others can produce more efficiently and skillfully than I. Outsourcing has allowed me to focus more time on the items I can proficiently produce.

It's not necessary to announce to your client or guests that a certain item was bought ready-made. If someone does ask outright "Did you make this?" all you need to say is "We hired experts to make it for us." No one will call the catering police.

Make Your Menu Look Just As BEAUTIFUL *as The Food On It*

When creating a printed menu to give to a client, make sure that it is clean, easy-to-read and that it showcases your creativity. Use colors and fonts that let your ideas shine through yet offers your client an intimate experience of the items you have suggested for her menu. Break down the sections clearly so that the menu demonstrates the flow of the event.

FOUR: GIVE PEOPLE WHAT THEY WANT

Idiosyncrasies

As a personal wish, some clients may want the menu to include some foods that have personal meaning to them. It could be a family recipe or something they love to cook themselves. I've even had shy kids produce recipes to feature at their own celebrations. Once a twelve-year-old created a knock-out menu item for a Red Sox-themed party: mini-cheeseburgers with spicy ketchup for fries. This was long before sliders had reached celebrity cuisine status. Talk about satisfied clients and guests! As much as clients are happy to hear your ideas and expertise, they are equally delighted to live their food creation dreams through you.

Food Costs

What should you do if your client feels that the menu just won't work without a particularly expensive item? There are clever ways to include costlier foods. For example, I had a client who desperately wanted caviar at her eightieth birthday party, but was also quite frugal. I really wanted to fulfill her vision, but initially couldn't imagine how I could provide this on her budget. Finally, I came up with the idea of a mini potato station with several reasonably priced caviars and other ingredients for fun optional toppings. She was thrilled. I had a staff person servicing the station to control the amount of caviar served on each potato, ensuring abundant caviar for all!

On the flip side, don't forget that items such as fresh spring herbs or a few hearts of palm can impress a group of guests. When added to

a simple green salad, these sort of items take that dish up quite a few
notches, creating something simple yet gourmet with practically no
extra cost. And when you save money on one area of the menu, you
can put it toward something that the client really wants—like caviar.

Current Food Trends and Fashions

Another way to make sure that you offer clients what they want
is to keep apprised of food trends, just as a clothing designer would
do. Even if you want to be known for your classics, or signature items,
you still may want to update your selections in light of current fads.
Fried food was considered a "never" with my client base when I began
catering. I would not have dreamed of suggesting a Louisiana fried
oyster for a quick passed appetizer. Yet, one day, about ten years into
the business, I saw a tasty corn fritter recipe in a magazine. Was it
possible that fried foods were coming back into fashion? I suggested
an assortment of fritters as part of a brunch menu, and the hostess
agreed. At the event, guests were lined up out the hall, coming back
for seconds. After this demonstration that fried foods were "in",
I began featuring them on my menus, albeit selectively.

Thanks to the basic law of supply and demand, it's true that fashionable often translates to costly. For example, the increasing popularity of the local food movement has resulted in clients seeking vegetables, fruits, cheeses and even meats produced on local farms, yet
these items cost a great deal more than their non-local counterparts.
If a client requests something trendy and pricey, or you believe it important to include such an item as part of your menu, discuss the costs
with your client at the onset of menu proposal. If the client really
wants it, they will not be deterred by the additional costs you will need
to charge.

Trendier does not always equal costlier, however, and if you keep
on top of food fashions you'll often come across popular items that
can be added to a menu at relatively low cost. Mini Belgian Waffles,
for example, are a cheap and easy item currently enjoying star status
at Miss Jeanies events. Hot-out-of-the-oven chocolate chip cookies,
served with milk in shot glasses, are another popular item that are very
inexpensive compared to many traditional desserts.

Guest Demographics

When planning your menu, you should always consider the demographics of your client and guests. Be sensitive to cultural differences. Where one culture may find an abundance of appetizers before
a plated dinner to be excessive, another may interpret an offering of
just two or three simple appetizers as withholding on the hostess'

part. Do your homework. You could even read ahead about the client's culture and subtly address it in your first meeting.

Also consider the age ranges of the guests. I've had elderly hostesses describe themselves as "adventurous eaters," yet their idea of an adventurous menu is different than that of a thirty-year-old adventurous eater. Spices and heat preferences would be different for these two groups. When a guest list spans a large range of ages, you should try to make certain that the menu includes some core foods acceptable and enjoyable by all. Then you can liven it up by adding sauces, salsas, appetizers or side dishes that appeal to different tastes.

So there you have it, the tools to begin planning your menu for your first job. Looking forward, you will learn how integral pricing is to developing and finalizing your menu. Your budget will ultimately determine what will and won't work in the end.

CHAPTER SEVEN
Pricing Your Menu and Event Staff

YOUR GOAL IN PRICING IS TO REACH A FAIR,
COMPETITIVE PRICE FOR YOUR CLIENT AND A
PROFITABLE PRICE FOR YOURSELF.

. . . .

Money doesn't buy happiness, but happiness doesn't stop you from needing money. When you first begin catering, you may be so pleased when your food is well-received and so fulfilled by the work you're doing that your pricing takes a back seat. In my "honeymoon period," I was so excited about my business ideas that I would do anything to realize them, even spend money from my hard-earned savings. Then, a year into my catering efforts, my husband asked if I was making any money from all my work. He was supportive of my business, but that didn't mean that it didn't create difficulties for him. He'd become responsible for driving weekend carpools, doing housework that I no longer had the time for, and loading and unloading the car for jobs. I *was* in fact making some money, but due to my disorganization, I had no numbers that I could proudly share with my husband. It was time to find a system for accurately pricing food and event staff.

There's more than one accepted system used for pricing in the catering industry, and it's up to you to decide which one you'll use. If you've had experience working for a large caterer or even a restaurant, you might find that the easiest route is to take what you learned and tailor it to your needs. Or you might have a preference for a certain method of money management, such as a specific software program, and find that this lends itself to a particular pricing system. As always, you want to do what works for you.

A key thing to remember as you read through this chapter is that **you will be pricing a job as part of creating an estimated budget**. Keep in mind the distinction between an estimated budget and a final bill. You'll need to do a lot of predicting and guessing in order to foresee the costs of an event that may be scheduled a year down the line. You'll also need to learn to do your pricing very quicky, as clients will often demand numbers on the spot (consider yourself lucky if you've got a day or two to draw up a budget).

In addition, specify on your policy sheet that a product's price may change by the time it is actually purchase for the event (See Chapter 9 for more on the Policy Sheet). These product costs are based on market fluctation and therefore unpredictable. For example, costs can be influenced by the price of gas, weather conditions, even unexpected natural disasters. Numbers estimated to the client one year could be as much as ten or twenty percent higher the next. Apprising your client of this on your policy sheet will protect you.

PRE-PRICING: CREATING A COST DATABASE

In order to prepare to price your menus, I suggest that you create a cost database that you'll be able to use as a reference. Begin by listing between 25 and 50 of the foods you use most often, such as flour, sugar, oils, chicken breasts, etc. Then list the price of each item at three different stores. Make sure that the quantities are consistent—you'll cause yourself a lot of headache if your database says that all three stores sell a bottle of balsamic vinegar for ten dollars, yet the three bottles are different sizes. To avoid such confusion, notate prices as a reflection of the item's weight, i.e. cents per ounce or dollars per pound.

Your database should also include specialty foods that feature often on your menus. It may be the case that you only have one choice of vendor for these—if so, you'll still want to note the cost of the item in your database, even if you aren't comparing the cost across stores.

A little technology goes a long way in creating your database. If you have a smartphone, you can install an app that allows you to scan the barcode of an item at the store. It will then provide you with the price of that same item at other retailers.

THE COST OF FOOD

For the purposes of this chapter, **I'm going to focus on the way I price menus at Miss Jeanies**. The first thing to note about my pricing system is that on my budget proposals (the numbers I actually show to clients), I separate the price of the Menu from the price of Event Staffing. How are these distinguished?

Menu refers to the cost of the food PLUS the cost of the pre-job labor that goes into producing the food (for instance, shopping, cooking and other prepwork).

Event Staffing refers to the work done at the event (ncluding getting the food packed up and transporting it to and from the event site).

The separation between these two categories provides my clients with transparency, giving them a better understanding of what they are paying for. Remember that you may be writing these proposals months or even years in advance of an event. In the intervening time, food and staff decisions will likely change, whether it's by my choice or that of the client. Having separate line items for Menu and Event Staffing makes it easier to accommodate the fluctuations that occur.

We'll be using the following menu as an example:

Kids' Lunch Menu for Fifty Guests

Creamy Tomato Soup - 1 Serving Per Guest, Total 50

Classic Grilled Cheeses - 2 Servings Per Guest, Total 100

Ice Cream Sandwiches - 2 Servings Per Guest, Total 100

We'll follow a four step process for costing out each item on the menu.

1. Review the Recipe
2. Convert the Recipe
3. Analyze the Quantity Information
4. Cost Out the Item

Keep in mind that at this point you're figuring out how much the food costs you to produce, not how much you'll charge the client. Ready?

Step 1: Review The Recipe

Creamy Tomato Sop
MAKES 5 SERVINGS

INGREDIENTS:

28 oz. Crushed Tomatoes   .5 cup Heavy Cream
2 Tbs. Olive Oil   1 Onion, Chopped
1.5 cups Chicken Stock

DIRECTIONS:

Pour olive oil into a medium stockpot over medium heat. Cook onion, stirring constantly, until soft and translucent, about 3 minutes.

Add tomatoes, their juices, and chicken stock. Bring to a boil, then reduce heat and simmer 10 minutes.

Working in batches, transfer tomato mixture to a blender, food processor, or food mill. Puree tomato mixture (if using a blender, cover the lid with a kitchen towel while machine is running).

Return soup to a clean pot and set over low heat. Season with your choice of spices. Serve immediately or transfer soup to a bowl set over an ice-water bath to cool completely. Transfer cooled soup to an airtight container and refrigerate. Reheat over medium heat.

Step 2: Convert The Recipe

If you're not familiar with how to convert a recipe to make more or fewer servings than the original would produce, it just requires some multiplication. Below, we convert the recipe for 5 servings of soup into a recipe for 50 servings of soup by multiplying each ingredient quantity by a factor of 10.

Ingredients for 5 Servings:	Ingredients for 50 Servings:
1 (28 oz.) can crushed tomatoes	10 (28 oz.) cans crushed tomatoes
1.5 Tbs Olive Oil	15 Tbs. or 7.5 oz Olive Oil
1 onion	10 onions
1.5 cups Chicken Stock	15 cups Chicken Stock
.5 cup Heavy Cream	5 cups Heavy Cream

Step 3: Analyze Quantity Information

To figure out exactly what you need to buy, you'll need to look at each ingredient and consider the quantities in which that ingredient is available. If the recipe uses 7.5 oz of olive oil, and a small bottle of olive oil contains 8 oz, you'll need to round up and buy a whole bottle, even though you won't use all of it. Review each ingredient and do whatever rounding is necessary to ensure you have enough. Also do any additional conversions necessary. For example, if your grocer prices onions by the pound (as opposed to by the individual onion), you'll need to know the approximate weight of an onion in order to figure out the cost of 10.

Quantity Analysis	Quantity to Buy
You buy tomatoes in 28 oz cans, as the recipe says.	10 cans
You need 7.5 oz olive oil; a bottle contains 8 oz.	1 bottle
A large onion weighs about 1 lb.	10 lbs.
Chicken stock is sold in quarts (4 cups to a quart)	4 quarts
Heavy cream is also sold by the quart	2 quarts

Step 4: Cost Out the Item

For each ingredient, use your price list to find the unit cost, then multiply to find the total cost.

	Unit Cost	Quantity	Total Cost
10 cans crushed tomatoes	$2.00 / can	10 cans	$20.00
1 bottle of olive oil	$4 / bottle	1 bottle	$4.00
10 lbs. of onions	$1 / lb.	10 lbs.	$10.00
4 quarts of chicken stock	$3.00 / quart	4 quarts	$12.00
2 quarts of heavy cream	$6.00 / quart	2 quarts	$12.00
		Subtotal: $58	

We can put this subtotal into a number of different formats:

Cost Per Serving: Dividing the subtotal by the total number of servings—50—will give you the cost per individual serving: $1.16

Cost Per Guest: Since each guest will have 1 serving of soup, the subtotal per guest will also be $1.16. We'll later try an example where each guest has more than one serving.

The next item on the menu is the Classic Grilled Cheese, with 2 sandwiches per guest. We'll go through the steps a little quicker this time.

Step 1: Review The Recipe

Classic Grilled Cheeses
MAKES 1 SERVING

INGREDIENTS:

2 Slices of Bread   2 oz. of sliced cheese   2 Tbs. Butter

DIRECTIONS:

Heat a non-stick griddle or a sandwich maker until hot.

Place 2 oz. of cheese on a slice of bread. Top with remaining bread slice, pressing gently to adhere. Generously butter both sides of the bread.

Place sandwich on the griddle. Cook until golden brown on each side and the cheese has completely melted, 3 to 4 minutes per side, turning once. Before removing from griddle, flip sandwiches to reheat first side, about 15 seconds. Cut each sandwich diagonally in half.

Step 2: Convert the Recipe

Ingredients for 1 Serving:	Ingredients for 100 Servings:
2 slices bread	200 slices bread
2 oz. of sliced cheese	200 oz. (12.5 lbs) sliced cheese
2 Tbs. butter	200 Tbs. (12.5 cups) butter

Step 3: Analyze Your Quantities

Quantity Analysis	Quantity to Buy
1 loaf of bread yields 10 slices.	20 loaves
Cheese is sold by weight. You need 12.5 pounds.	12.5 pounds
A stick of butter yields 0.5 cup. You need 12.5 cups.	25 sticks

Lending to and Borrowing From Your Stock

Let's introduce a new idea. You need 25 sticks of butter. A stick of butter, bought by itself, costs $1.25. Since it's always a better value to buy in larger quantities, you want to avoid buying 25 individual sticks of butter. Luckily, your local bulk retailer sells a box that contains 8 sticks of butter and costs $6.40.

• If you buy three such boxes, you have 24 sticks—too little.

• If you buy four of these boxes, you'll have 32 sticks, which is more than you need for this recipe.

But butter is always a good thing to have on hand, right? So you decide it's worth it to buy the four 8-packs, which runs you $25.60. Divide that by 32 to see that you're paying $0.80 a stick.

When you cost out your butter, you'll notate it as 25 sticks of butter at $0.80 a stick, or a total of $20.00.

However, you still had to pay $25.60 at the store. So how does this work? You've just lent your business $5.60 worth of butter. The idea is that when you need butter for a future recipe, you'll have it on hand—you'll then be able to borrow it from your business. You won't have to buy anything new, but when you cost out that future item, you'll still cost out the butter at $.80 per stick, not at $0. Eventually, it will even out like this:

Kid's Lunch Menu: Costed out butter at $20.00, or $.80 a stick.
Lent business stock $5.60 worth of butter.

Future Menu: Borrowed 7 sticks of butter ($5.60 worth) from stock.
Costed out butter at $5.60 total, or $.80 a stick.

Why pay $1.25 a stick when you can pay $0.80? Be savvy and save!

Step 4: Cost Out the Item

	Unit Cost	Quantity	Total Cost
20 loaves of bread	$3 / loaf	20 loaves	$60
12.5 pounds of cheese	$7.20 / pound	12.5 lbs.	$90
25 sticks of butter	$0.80 / stick	25 sticks	$20

Subtotal: $170 total
Cost Per Serving: $1.70
Cost Per Guest: $3.40

Note that because the menu calls for more than one serving per guest, the cost per serving is no longer equal to the cost per guest.

Now we're on to the ice cream sandwiches.

Step 1: Review the Recipe

Ice Cream Sandwiches
MAKES 20 SERVINGS

INGREDIENTS:

2.5 pounds pre-made Sugar Cookie Dough
10 cups Ice Cream

DIRECTIONS:

Portion pre-made cookie dough into forty 1 oz balls, and place on a lined cookie tray. Bake until the edges are just slightly golden, about 10 minutes.

Remove cookies from the oven and let cool for 15 minutes. When cookies are completely cooled, scoop a 1/2 cup of ice cream atop the flat side of one cookie. Top with another cookie. Refreeze.

Step 2: Convert the Recipe

The above recipe makes 20 ice cream sandwiches, and you need 100. Therefore multipy by a factor of five.

Ingredients for 20 Servings:	Ingredients for 100 Servings:
2.5 pounds cookie dough	12.5 pounds cookie dough
10 cups Ice Cream	50 cups Ice Cream

Step 3: Analyze Your Quantities

A bulk dealer sells 20 lb. tub of cookie dough. It will yield many more cookies than you need, but we'll cover that on the following page.

Quantity Analysis	Quantity to Buy
A 20 lb. tub of cookie dough yields 320 cookies.	1 tub
Ice cream can be bought by the gallon. A gallon	4 gallons
is equivalent to 16 cups.	

We just went over how you can loan foods like butter to your business stock, thus making use of the extras and allowing you to only charge the client for the amount you use. You can also borrow items from your business stock. With this recipe, say that you have almost a full tub of cookie dough leftover from a previous job. You can borrow 12.5 lbs of cookie dough from that tub, therefore only charging your client for what you use. With other foods, however, you will have to charge your client for the entire quantity that you buy, even if you don't use it all. For this recipe, you needed 50 cups of Ice Cream. A gallon is equivalent to 16 cups: therefore, 3 gallons (48 cups) won't be sufficient. You'll have to buy 4 gallons (64 cups), leaving you with about 14 extra cups of ice cream. If you have no immediate use for that extra ice cream (unlike the butter, which you could easily use), **it's acceptable to charge the client for all 4 gallons of ice cream. Whether or not you do so is up to you.** You'll also encounter this scenario with foods that will spoil quickly, or with specially-requested foods that you don't foresee needing on any upcoming menus.

Step 4: Cost Out the Item

	Unit Cost	Quantity	Total Cost
12.5 lbs. cookie dough	$80 for 20 lb. tub	$5/8$ of a tub	$50
4 gallons of ice cream	$7 / gallon	4 gallons	$28

Subtotal: $78
Cost Per Serving: $0.78
Cost Per Guest: $1.56

So what's the total cost of the food for the Kid's Lunch menu?

50 Servings Creamy Tomato Soup..$58
100 Grilled Cheese Sandwiches $170
100 Ice Cream Sandwiches: $78
Grand Total..$306

That's the cost of the **food** on the menu. We can also state that as $6.12 a head. But don't forget that the cost of the menu includes not just food but pre-job labor costs. We're coming up to that next.

THE COST OF PRE-JOB LABOR

Next you will want to conduct a cost analysis to determine your pre-job labor costs. To do this, you must figure out approximately how long it will take to plan, shop, prepare, cook, and store the food items on your menu. Back in Chapter 4, one of our To-Dos suggested that you observe how long it actually takes you to perform various tasks. As another exercise, take a few of your proposed menu items—adjusted for quantity—and break down the steps in great detail. This might help you realize just how much time is involved in preparing a "simple" recipe when you have to both cook it in large quantities and put it away so it can be served later.

So, how long would it take to make our Kids' Lunch menu?

=============== | Creamy Tomato Soup | ===============

Get out all ingredients you will be using. Measure out the quantities of each item for 50 servings. Chop Onions .... 25 min

Take out stockpot and pour in olive oil. Add chopped onions. Stir for 3 minutes. Add tomatoes, juices and stock; bring to boil .... 10 min

Reduce heat and simmer. While the soup is simmering, clean up your kitchen and get out your supplies for the next step. Take out a clean pot and put it on the stove .... 10 min

Transfer soup in batches to food processor and return to new pot after processing. Season with any spices to taste. Do not add cream unless you are serving immediately .... 25 min

Set the soup over low heat . During this time, clean up food processor and either get the ice water bath ready or prepare for bringing soup to the refrigerator. If not using an ice bath, turn off the burner and let the soup sit on the stove until cools down for 30 or so minutes. (During this time you will begin to get the ingredients ready for your next task,) .... 30 min

Make sure soup has cooled down to about 40 degrees. Cover the soup with foil or plastic wrap, placing it in the refrigerator, making sure not to place it near other ingredients whose safety could be hurt by raising their temperature (see Chapter 11 for more on Food Safety) .... 10 min

Total Time: 110 minutes or 1 $5/6$ hours

Classic Grilled Cheeses

Get out your appropriate quantitites and all your ingredients .... 15 minutes

Prep 200 slices of bread with designated quantities of cheese and butter. Place one slice of bread on top of another .... 100 minutes

Heat the pan or skillet and start making sandwiches, assuming you can make 4 at a time (If you use multiple skillets, you can do more at once). At this rate, it will take you 25 rounds to cook your 100 sandwiches. And each round takes about 5 minutes to cook .... 125 minutes.

Total Time: .... 240 minutes or 4 hours

Ice Cream Sandwiches

Defrost cookie dough .... 15 minutes

Form cookie dough into a hundred 1-oz balls .... 30 minutes

Bake off 4 trays of cookies, baking 2 trays at a time. Each tray will go in the oven for 10 minutes .... 20 minutes

Let cookies cool for 15 minutes. Scoop a ½ scoop of ice cream between the flat sides of two cookies .... 30 minutes

Place cookies back in freezer .... 5 minutes

Total Time: 100 minutes or 1 2/3 hours

Grand Total (for cooking this menu 1 item at a time): 7.5 HRS

Obviously, you will save a lot of time by learning to multitask. Some tasks require utmost concentration: take your eye off the grill, and your sandwiches may burn. But if you have a slow soup simmering on the stove, that might be a good time to start portioning out your cookies. When your cookies are in the oven, it might be a good time to slice the grilled cheese sandwiches. Your ultimate goal is to learn the best order in which to prepare your menu items so as to minimize the time required. If you're making a turkey that has to cook for 3 hours, get it ready first, then do whatever else you can while that is going on.

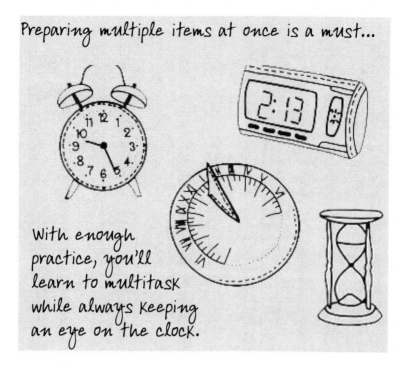

Preparing multiple items at once is a must...

With enough practice, you'll learn to multitask while always keeping an eye on the clock.

Figuring Out Pay Rates

Regardless of whether you're working solo, as you will likely be intially, or working with staff, you should determine an hourly rate for your own labor. If you're at the point in your business where you've hired staff to help you cook, you'll still pay yourself hourly, but your different staff members will likely be paid different hourly rates. Let's say you hire your sister to help prep and make the grilled cheese sandwiches (4 hours) and your teenage nephew to do the shopping (1 hour). You personally take on the responsibility of making the tomato soup and the ice cream sandwiches (110 minutes to make the soup + 100 minutes to make the ice cream sandwiches = 210 minutes, or 3.5 hours.)

You: 3.5 hours cooking at $24/hour..$84
Your Sister: 4 hours cooking @ $20/hour $80
Your Nephew: 1 hour shopping at @ $15/hr $15

Total Cost for Pre-Job Labor: $179
Now we have a total cost for Pre-Job Labor ($179) and a total cost for Food on the menu ($306), The next step is to price the event staff.

EVENT STAFF

Clients don't realize how many people are really needed to make a party work. In fact, they often significantly underestimate the number of staff it will take to fully realize their vision of the event. Early on in my business, I staffed in accordance with the client's sense of how many people were needed and boy, did we pay for it. We were often left breathless and extraordinarily stressed during the entire event.

As time went on, I developed my own sense of how many staff were needed for a job. Now most clients will defer to my judgement, especially after I run through a scenario or two that demonstrates just how many people it took to pull off an event. Some clients, however, will remain skeptical. They will ask me to justify the numbers I've suggested. If this happens with one of your clients, hang in there. Tell them that **the only way to provide the best service is to have the right number of staff working the party**. Tell them that although the proposed number of staff may seem high, there are many times in an event when it's critical to have "many hands in many places." Describe a moment at a cocktail party: two people passing appetizers, a chef heating appetizers at the stove, another staff plating the upcoming salad course, yet another prepping food for the main course. Prior to this example, your client may have insisted you need three staff members, but you clearly need at least five.

How do you begin to estimate the number of staff needed and how much to charge for them? Start with a mental dress rehearsal of the entire event. Picture packing up for your job. Picture all that happens after the arrival at the site: kitchen set-up, cooking, serving, clean up. Picture loading and unloading at the end of the event. Consider that extra help is often worth its cost in the increased efficiency it provides.

I have read articles on catering that suggest using a staff-to-guest ratio to calculate how many staff to schedule. I have never found such formulas useful, because staffing needs are not that cut and dried. There are often additional details that need to be factored into your staff pricing:

- Is there anything specific the client has requested done that will take extra time or hands?

- Is there a kitchen? Do you need to set one up? Will you need to clean and arrange the existing kitchen when you arrive?

- Is it a sit-down meal or a buffet?

- How long before the event can you arrive at the site, and how long after can you remain? Are your set-up or clean-up periods limited?

Another aspect to consider when scheduling your staff is that all staff does not need to arrive at the party at the same time. You can begin with a small core group who unloads the car, moves items into the site, and gets started. Then, depending on the kitchen and the set-up demands of the job, you can stagger staff arrivals. Once I've established my core staff schedule, I will have serving staff arrive closer to "show-time." Clients appreciate this method, because it avoids a scenario where excess staff members end up standing around with nothing to do. Estimate carefully, though: it is far preferable to have abundant staff on hand than to experience the terrible crunch of barely getting the job done.

If you have a non-core group of staff that only works at the peak of the party, some of these staff members may only end up working for an hour or two. This won't be possible, however, if you establish a "Staff Minimum," which many caterers in the industry do. If you establish a staff minimum of 5 hours, for example, and a client holds a party that only lasts 3 hours, they still have to pay each staff member for 5 hours. By not having a staff minimum, I can stagger my staff, thus satisfy both staff members who only want to work a short shift and clients who want to save on staff costs.

So, how much will you want to pay your staff? In the beginning of your business, it's more than likely that your staff will be just a friend or a sibling who is willing to help you out on a Saturday afternoon. If you get to the point where you keep staff on payroll, you will have costs such as health care, unemployment insurance, and Social Security. **To cover such expenses, you will need to charge the client more than what you pay your staff members** (see Chapter 13 for more). A company may charge a client $30 an hour per staff member, for instance, but they'll keep $10 of every $30 in order to cover things like payroll taxes and employee benefits.

Back to our Kid's Lunch scenario: you, your sister, and your nephew will be the core staff, and you'll each work four hours. Your nephew's girlfriend will work as a server for two hours at the peak of the party (Sidenote: it is acceptable to pay a staff member who works both pre-job and at the event different rates for these two services, but we don't do that here). So here is the event staff breakdown:

You: 4 hours at $25/hour $100
Your Sister: 4 hours @ $20/hour $80
Your Nephew: 4 hours @ $15/hr $60
Your Nephew's Girlfriend: 2 hours @ $15/hr $30

EVENT STAFFING COSTS: $270

FROM COST TO PRICE:
HOW MUCH WILL YOU CHARGE FOR THE MENU?

We know now how much it will *cost* for the menu (which, as a reminder, includes food costs and pre-job labor) and for the event staffing. The next step is to determine the price estimate that you will charge your client for these two things.

The industry standard is to take your food plus pre-job labor costs and multiply these times 3. This is known as the X3 Formula.

Food Costs + Pre-Job Labor Costs x 3 = Price You Will Charge Your Client for the Menu

So for the menu we've been using:

$306 food costs + $179 pre-job labor costs = $485
$485 x 3 = $1455
$1455 = Menu Price

It can be as simple as that, and this is where I suggest you start out pricing your jobs. You can charge the client $1455 and call it a day. There's just one problem: the price works out to $29.10 per guest, and **that's not including the cost of event staff** (which brings the cost up by $240!) Almost thirty dollars a head! That's steep for a kid's party. If you believe that your client will accept this budget without batting an eye, then by all means, charge them accordingly. If not, it may be necessary to deviate from the X3 formula in order to find a price that works for you and your client. Welcome to Pricing Your Menu, Level 2: Subtle Nuances and Variables.

SUBTLE NUANCES AND VARIABLES

We'll now go through the subtle nuances and variables that may compel you to deviate from the X3 formula, either by raising or lowering your prices. For instance, say you really want to cater the Kid's Lunch. The party will be held during your slow season and furthermore, the client is her school's PTO President, making her a great potential source of referrals. These sort of factors might serve as incentive to lower your prices to meet her budget.

On the other end of the spectrum, what if the client has told you that another caterer gave her an estimate of $40 a plate? And what if it's a rush job? Those sorts of factors can help justify the $30/plate price, or even give you cause to bump the price!

Fixed Overhead

Fixed overhead—your rent, utilities, insurances, etc.—comes into play when and if you rent space to produce your products. Fixed overhead refers to expenses that you must pay every month no matter how much business you do that month. What many small business owners do in order to guesstimate their expenses for the year to come is review their fixed overhead for the past year and divide that figure by the number of jobs they had that past year. Over the next year, they'll add that amount to each job to cover their fixed overhead.

Variable Overhead

From the day you begin your business, you'll incur expenses such as stamps, gasoline, stationary, photocopying, printer cartridges, and more. I would not worry about these at first: if you follow the X3 formula, you will probably be making enough to cover these.

As your business grows, you will want to have a sense of how much your spend annually on variable overhead. Each year this amount may change. One year you may have a reduced need for stamps or printer cartridges because you begin to send all your bills and proposals electronically, but you may need a new computer or scanner. If you anticipate needing extra funds for variable overhead one year, you may wish to divide the cost of the budgeted item(s) across the jobs you have scheduled for the year, thus ensuring that you'll earn enough to cover your costs.

A Client's Non-Negotiable Budget

This only happens once in a while, but I actually like it when it does. I use the X3 formula and see how close the result comes to the amount the client wishes to pay. If it is close, that's fabulous. I either raise the price up to her budget, or leave the price a little under her budget (clients are rarely unhappy about this). However, if the price I get using the X3 formula is significantly higher than the client's budget, I have two options. I can accept a smaller profit on this job, which I might do when there's an advantage to taking the job (With the Kid's Lunch, for instance, the client's potential as a great referreal source is a definite advantage). Alternatively, I can go back to the client and suggest that we tweak her menu to stay within her budget. This could mean leaving off an item or two, or suggesting a similar menu that will allow you to offer her a price in line with her budget. Communicate that you would really like to work this out with her, and you'll most likely be able to agree on a menu that will work for both of you.

The Kind Of Party Being Given

It's amazing, but identical menus can be priced differently depending upon the kind of occasion and the client's perception of that occasion. For example, the same menu may be served at a Saturday evening birthday party at a client's home and at a wedding held in a rented function hall. Your food costs and pre-event labor costs may be identical, but the wedding menu can still be priced higher than the birthday party menu. Crazy, but true. Although this practice is an industry norm, it will be up to you to decide how you want to alter your price in these situations.

Another nuance related to client perception is colloquially known as "snob pricing." Some clients "need" to pay a loftier price in order to believe that they are receiving a superb product. The price determined by using your X3 formula may actually sound too low to your client. In order to get the job, raise your price. Your client will have confidence that they're getting the best of the best, and you'll make extra profit.

The Turn Around Time For The Party

Most of my jobs are scheduled months ahead. On occasion, however, I will get a call requesting that an event be thrown together quickly. If I am not overly busy, I may say yes. I would feel justified in taking the X3 formula and adding to the result to compensate for the pressure of getting the shopping, food prep and delivery done on the spur of the moment. Clients understand that this is a fair charge for their "last minute need."

The Opportunities the Job May Bring

This is an interesting call that you will become more sophisticated in making as time goes on. If a job promises to lead to other jobs in the future, but the client's budget is below the X3 formula, is it worth it to accept a decreased profit?

In the early years, I rarely turned down any jobs, even if a client's stated budget was significantly below the X3 formula. My hope was that all jobs were opportunities to land other jobs. This was probably a smart philosophy. Now, years later, unless I anticipate that showing goodwill toward the client will bring in more jobs, I'll say "no thank you" when the client's budget is below the X3. These days, I also say "no thank you" more often because I am more confident that referrals will come from *somewhere*, regardless of whether I take on a particular job. I'd rather save my time and energy for jobs that pay at least as much as the X3 amount.

Another risk of offering your job for a lower price is that this client may enthusiastically tell her friends and colleagues of her negotiated price, and they will expect the same "special price." Five referrals later, you may still be expected to offer this rate to other clients.

Things to Consider...

Keeping Your Pricing Structure Private

Despite the fact that you use a straightforward method to arrive at your price, I don't recommend revealing your system to a client. Even though there have been times I've felt compelled to offer up my pricing methodology when a client reacts negatively to my price, I've rarely seen this end well. Better that you reconfigure your menu, offering it in a way that costs you less. I feel there's something about the catering business that needs to remain a little magical, and pricing is a good place to start.

Yet another risk of lowering your price is that if the client gets wind that you're charging less than normal, she may suspect that your normal prices are inflated, and that the "deal" you're giving her isn't a deal at all.

In my opinion, **the one scenario in which it's always safe to lower your price without fearing negative fallout is for repeat customers**. If I am catering the third or fourth party for a client or for someone who has referred clients to me, I often will reduce the price. I'll let them know that I'm doing this as a token of my gratitude for their loyal and continuing support.

The Competition for the Job

Referrals for Miss Jeanies tend to come from generations of clients who have either attended a party we've catered or know someone who has. When prospective clients call, they are fairly certain that they want to work with us, as long as the price we offer ends up close enough to their budget. But sometimes, I can detect that a new client only wants to know what I'll charge her to get leverage. There's another caterer who she'd prefer to work with, and she wants to show my number to them in hopes that they'll bring down their price.

I've never enjoyed bidding on jobs that I know other caterers are bidding on. In part, the "one of a kind" character of the Miss Jeanies brand makes it hard for me to price the way other caterers are pricing. It's just not "apples" and "apples." I offer a great deal of customization and special client services. Additionally, bidding against other caterers can cause me to offer my jobs at prices lower than I would like. I don't want to lower my price ahead of time based simply on the guess that other companies may offer lower prices. To me, this feels more like gambling and less like relationship building. Your style of competitiveness may make you feel differently, and that's perfectly legitimate as well.

The Economic Environment

As I mentioned in Chapter 3, catering is considered to be relatively recession proof. What I have found with my business is that regardless of the economic environment, people continue to celebrate milestones, companies still hold staff parties, special occasions still arise. However, budgets become a little tighter when the economy is down. Even if the clients themselves are financially secure enough that they don't *have* to alter their budget, the psychology of the economic times appears to affect their decision making. If the culture in which they live advocates frugality, clients will follow that cue. It's considered tacky to be ostentatious when those around are out of work or wondering how they'll pay the bills.

The Luxuriousness of Items on the Menu

Public perception is that luxury food items cost more, so clients expect a caterer or restaurant to charge more for such products. I don't think this is true. The best example for what I've termed "The Myth of the Catering Market" is beef tenderloin. Just mention "beef tenderloin" and your client will squirm.

Which do you think costs more for a caterer to produce as an entrée: crabcakes or beef tenderloin? It's the crabcakes, as you've probably guessed. Let's break it down.

- Beef tenderloin costs me $8.99/lb. Each pound yields 3 servings. My pre-job labor time (seasoning and searing it) to make 10 pounds of tenderloin—enough to serve 30 people—is about 30 minutes.
- A large crabcake costs $2, and there are 2 crab cakes in a serving. To serve 30 people, I'd need to make 60 crabcakes. The pre-job labor time for that is about 2 hour.

If I charge $20/hour for my labor, then the math looks like this:

Tenderloin:	30 servings @ $3/serving costs **$90** +	.5 hour @ $20/hr costs **$10** =	$100 total for 30 guests =	$3.33 per guest
Crabcakes:	30 servings @ $4/serving costs **$120** +	2 hours @ $20/hr costs **$40** =	$160 total for 30 guests =	$5.33 per guest

I could show this to you with countless other comparisons: a chicken dish versus a tenderloin, a shrimp dish versus a chicken dish, etc. The bottom line is that you can decide whether you want to allow the false cost perception of the luxury items to allow you to charge more despite your real costs. Doing so is certainly industry standard, but as always, do what you see fit.

The Number of Guests

True or false: If you double the number of guests, your food and labor costs are 2 times as great. False!

Think about it: it does not take you two times as long to cook for ten guests as it does for five. Mixing up the spices, stirring the pot, and washing the dishes takes nearly the same amount of time. Your shopping time stays nearly exact. Yes, your food costs will increase somewhat, but for most items, they will not double. Knowing this reality, different caterers price their jobs differently. Some caterers will welcome the extra incremental money earned for each additional guest. Others will not.

But this is all so complicated!

Yes, it is. There's no denying that. But with time and practice, your pricing will become increasingly sophisticated. The true brilliance of catering is figuring out how to produce the most special menu possible at the ideal cost. When you figure these out, you are in control of your menu. This will make you comfortable addressong other aspects of your event.. read onto to find out how.

RECIPE REQUIREMENT: Something that you can
Make Ahead and Freeze

Making a menu item ahead of time and freezing it: it's oh so tempting, but is it "legal?" Absolutely, as long as the menu items are right. This appetizer is so easy to make, and once out it's out of the way, you can focus on other menu items that demand last minute prep. Experiment with this versatile recipe by switching the cheddar for blue cheese, smoked gouda, or any other favorites.

Cheddar Pecan Biscuits

INGREDIENTS:
¾ cup butter (at room temperature)
1½ cups extra sharp cheddar cheese (grated)
¼ cup grated parmesan cheese
1 ½ cups all purpose flour
1 tsp salt
pinch cayenne pepper
½ cup finely chopped pecans
assorted toppings

Combine the butter and cheese in food processor until smooth.

Pour the flour, salt and cayenne pepper dirently into the food processor and process until the mixture begins to form a ball.

Add the pecans and gently pulse to integrate. Mixture will be soft but will hold together.

Make logs about 1 inch in diameter and place on a cookie tray. Put in freezer until the day you want to serve.

On the day they'll be served, let logs defrost in your refrigerator. Cut them into ¼ inch slices and place on cookie sheets with parchment paper.

Bake at 350° F for about 10 minutes, turning over once. Biscuits should be light golden brown.

When biscuits have cooled slightly, top with jam, soft cheeses, finely chopped nuts, or anything else you like.

CHAPTER EIGHT
Services Beyond Food and Staff

IF YOU'RE GOING TO PROVIDE EVENT SERVICES
OTHER THAN FOOD AND STAFF, YOU NEED TO
KNOW WHAT TO OFFER— AND HOW TO PRICE IT.

We've spent a lot of time discussing how food and event staffing costs can be calculated in order to set a menu price. Sometimes this is all your client will hire you to do: provide wonderful food and staff for an event. But I have found that more often than not, clients will ask you to provide additional services as part of a catering job. When I first began in the business, I wasn't prepared for such requests. I thought that the job description of a caterer was to provide food and staffing, period. Yet in keeping with client demand, I eventually began coordinating beverages, rentals, décor, and other aspects of an event.

There are innumerable scenarios when it comes to the division of labor between a client, a caterer, and third parties. Sometimes, clients begin by hiring an event planner and the *caterer* is a third party, hired by the event planner to provide food and event staff for a party. Under this scenario you would provide a menu that works well with the client and event planner's vision. It is also possible that you could be asked to handle only one or two of the event planning services, such as creating a "non-alcoholic drink table" with creative beverages. Regardless of the specifics of the arrangement, sooner or later you'll probably be asked to take care of one or more of the following:

Bartender	Beverages
Rentals	Paper Products
Décor and Design	Invitations
Photographer/Videographer	Music
Additional Entertainment	Valet Services

But I Didn't Sign Up For This!

You get to decide whether you want to take on any
event-planning responsibilities. Maybe you want to stop
at designing and cooking a fabulous meal, or you just don't
have the time to spare while working part-time at another job
or raising young children. If this is the case, you are certainly
free to decline should a client asks you to provide additional
services. It's important to be able to offer the client other
options by having a list of vendors or event planners
who do good work and to whom you can
comfortably refer your client.

PRICING

Now is not the time or place for me to go into detailed guidelines
for pricing beyond food and staff. Let's just quickly go over a few key
concepts. If "event planner" was your primary job description, you'd
typically adhere to industry standards when it comes to pricing other
services. But you're not: you're a caterer whose repertoire includes
event planning services. You therefore have a little bit of wiggle room.
You will have to decide for yourself when you'll charge the same as
an event planner would charge, when you'll cut your client a deal, and
when you'll charge more.

Charge for Everything

For many caterers, the entire point of offering event planning services is to reap extra profits. The first way this is done is
by marking up prices on products. A glass of lemonade that you
can make for $.10 can be priced at $1.00 per glass. Cans of Coke
that you may get on sale for $.25 each can be priced at $2.00. A caterer may spend $100 at a flower market, create 20 centerpieces
out of those flowers, and charge the client $20 per centerpiece.

In addition, **for each service that you coordinate for a client, you can earn a service charge.** For example, if your client wants to use an outside florist, you are allowed to charge your client for the work you do in making the referral and managing the service, even if the client herself arranges the details with the florist. You made the referral after all, and it will be you that has to follow through with the logistics, making certain that the flowers arrive at the event and are set up correctly before the party begins. Even if the florist were to bill the client directly, you could add a charge to your bill for your efforts.

Actually, Don't Charge for Everything

Sometimes it is to your advantage to only charge a nominal fee for a service. For example, if a separate bartending company is taking care of alcoholic beverages and soft drinks, but you're preparing fruited waters in pitchers, iced tea, and lemonades, you can just add on a nominal fee, a gesture of "goodwill" to your client.

You may also wish to refrain from excess surcharges when renting speciality equipment to your client. If your niche is defined by foods that require certain equipment, clients probably shouldn't incur extra fees for requesting such offerings. If your business, "Carnival Catering," is known for using old-fashioned popcorn machines and cotton candy makers at events, do not charge the client extra to rent such items. You're providing one of your core products, not an above-and-beyond service.

BARTENDING

A good bartender makes a good bar and a good bar makes a good party. Guests go to the bar expecting good nature and good cheer, and a professional bartender makes sure to generate not only a tasty drink, but good spirit. On the rare occasion that I have worked with a bartender with a bad attitude, minimal interest, or insufficient knowledge of his product, I've seen the negative vibe impact the entire party

Before we talk about offering bartending as an additional service, let's talk about staying out of bartending. If you do elect to bow out of anything related to your client's bar, you should still discuss the details of the bar with your client before the event. Make sure she has obtained all of the elements necessary to set up the bar (buckets for ice under bar, ice, corkscrews, tables, tablecloths, etc.) as well as adequate quantities. Even if the client or event planner has hired a bartending service that should be taking care of these things, it doesn't hurt to remind the client of what they'll need. On the day of your job, you will be busy setting up the floor and getting your food ready, so it can throw off your carefully designed schedule if all of a sudden there is no ice.

> Looking the Part....
>
> ## Bartender Attire
>
> Perhaps the most visible wait staff, bartenders should dress well, wearing a tuxedo shirt or nice dress shirt and tie. You can either set the dress code yourself or coordinate it with the bartending service.

Who Will Serve the Liquor?

The first thing you need to determine with regards to offering bartending is whether you want to have a bartender on your staff, in which case you will need to carry liquor liability insurance—no ifs, ands, or buts. Liquor liability—a significant issue in the catering and event industry—means that **you are responsible for a guest's behavior and safety if you or your staff has served them liquor.** If someone you have served leaves the party and gets into an accident, you could be deemed responsible and sued for damages. And "serving" is very widely defined in such cases. If your staff is running a smoothie bar, and a guest whips out a flask of tequila and says "Make it a non-virgin, will you?" you become liable. I therefore believe that even early on in your catering business, it is preferable to not take chances and expose yourself to liquor liability, which means hiring an outside bartender, rather than having one of your staff members bartend.

I recommend that you explain these issues when discussing bartending in the first meeting with your client. You can also suggest that a client investigate their homeowner's insurance policy: homeowner's insurance will usually provide liquor liability coverage, although liability coverage is typically limited to $100,000 to $300,000, depending on the policy. If they do have coverage, then you should offer to find a person for *them* to hire as a bartender. This will protect you from any liquor liability.

Be aware that many clients will push to have no bartender or will want to maintain their own bar. This can be a problem when the unattended bar becomes unkempt and needs replenishing as a party progresses. If a partygoer flags one of your staff members and asks them to grab another bottle of wine from the fridge, and your staff member complies, you become liable. You need to decide how strict you will be: will you let your staff members comply with the guests' requests? Or should your staff members play it safe and refuse to touch any alcohol, at the risk of aggravating the guests or even the client?

Clients will frequently have an opinion on how well they want to service their bar. Some are laid-back and don't mind their guests waiting in line for a drink, while others shudder at the thought. Others will want to spend more on bartenders than on the food-serving staff. Once you know where your client wants the bar staff to be on the scarce-abundant spectrum, you need to do some calculating. The bartending service we use most often suggests one bartender for every 40-50 guests, depending on the scenario of the party. You will need to consider pacing, too. Think about the beginning of a party when there is a rush to the bar—during this crunch time, you will need more bartenders. The bar will slow down as guests finish their first drink and circle back to the bar at their leisure. One solution for the early rush is the "express wine" option, where the bartender pours wine right before the party begins so that guests can quickly grab a glass, avoiding a wait in line at the bar.

What To Serve

It's important that you establish a bar that is fun, festive, and creative. Where once a "classic bar" was all my clients requested, these days I am finding they are increasingly interested in their bar being as creative as their food menu! When I think about the Gestalt of the party, I consider both the bar menu and the food menu, making certain there is a synchronicity between the two. If we are catering a summer BBQ, I include fun Texas beers. If it's a sophisticated cocktail party, I research the latest nightclub drinks and suggest them to my client. Frankly, one could make a whole career working with caterers to create bar drinks that coordinate with foods.

Another consideration is glassware and accessories. A whole new world of creative bartending has opened up over the past decade, with catering magazines and websites currently advertising creative glassware as well as stirrers, straws, toothpicks, and plastic ware. I believe that a decorative glass or fun stirrer can complement the individuality of a party and go a long way toward turning hydration into a hard-to-replicate moment.

As for creating garnishes to accompany drinks, the sky's the limit. You could stick to the classic lemons, limes and cocktail olives or get creative with something like a Bloody Mary garnished with sticks of pickles, celery, olives, green onions, and pickled vegetables.

Liquor Costs

New clients are often terrified that they'll need to mortgage their house to pay for a bar that serves anything other than beer. One of my happiest moments as a caterer comes when I can disavow clients of this commonly held misassumption. It's simple: **a bar need only cost the sum of the bottles that your client chooses.** If they choose an $8.00 bottle of wine and they go through 10 bottles, the bar bill will be $80. Yes, it adds up, but not to the extraordinary sums we are used to when we go to a restaurant or hotel and order drinks.
When helping my clients with their bar needs, I refer them to liquor stores that I know are honest, reliable, and fairly priced.

Some large catering companies handle their bar differently in order to increase their profit. They charge a "corking fee" per guest and/or mark up their liquor. Of course, they must maintain liquor liability insurance; they also face other complexities. As your company grows, you may want to look into this as a potential profit area.

BEVERAGES

Sometimes clients enjoy providing their own beverages. I have to admit that after years of catering, I am actually happy when I get a break from transporting dozens of extra bottles. But non-alcoholic beverage service is a frequent client request, and frankly, an easy way to increase your profit. As with your bar, you can decide how involved you will be with providing non-alcohol beverages and how you will want to charge for the service. There is no exact formula, but time and experience will help you figure it out.

Like alcoholic beverages, non-alcoholic beverages can serve as an expression of creativity at a party. Depending on the event, your client may just want the standard Coke products. You can also offer tap water infused with different fruits and herbs in elegant glass pitchers. You can also really add pizazz by putting together a creative refreshment that ties into the theme of the event. Don't forget that beverages can include hot drinks as well as cold ones. A Hot Chocolate Bar with different candies and marshmallows on skewers can bring a spark of warm energy to a cold winter's event.

RENTALS

    I briefly mentioned rentals in Chapter 5 when discussing the topics that should come up in your first meeting with your client. Rentals include tableware, glasses, linens, tables and chairs, percolators—everything needed to execute the party that you do not own yourself. You can even "rent" some of items you do own to your client instead of letting the client use them free of charge. I bet you didn't know the variety of items you can rent for a client that will entitle you to a mark-up or service charge. Couches, ottomans, furniture, backdrops, lighting, sound systems, vases, lamps, coat racks, even live plants—you name it—they're all available for rental.

    If there is any part of coordinating an event that requires utmost attention to detail, it is rentals. There is nothing more stressful than getting to your job and finding you ordered one less round tablecloth than neccessary or five fewer forks. How about forgetting a percolator when the hostess wants coffee served right from the beginning of her luncheon? Before letting the rental company know what you need, you must clearly think through all scenarios of the party, determining every item necessary to make it work. I frequently wake up early on the morning of an event, while the house is totally quiet, and think through every aspect of the party, step by step. I look at the floor plan and consider every tablecloth and pitcher, double-and-triple checking my notes.

    Most towns or cities have at least two competing rental companies that offer china, glassware, silver, table linens and basic equipment such as microwaves and convection ovens. I recommend getting the lay of the land by contacting these companies ahead of your first job. If you don't have this opportunity, don't worry: you can establish yourself with them and learn how their particular system works when you place your first order.

    Industry standard dictates that caterers are typically entitled to a 10% below-retail discount. Part of the reason for this discount is that it is easier for rental companies to work with professionals. In fact, many rental companies will not rent to the public and will require customers to rent through their caterers. I agree that **it is better for a caterer to do the renting than for the client to attempt it**. When a client tries to do their own rentals, they either get stressed over quantities and selections, or approach the rentals with a nonchalant, stress-free attitude, which results in disaster! When *I* do the rentals for a client, I have the assurance that we will have what we need at the event and I avoid a potential crisis the day of the party.

Event Essentials, Ltd.
19 August Street, Wilmington. DE 19801

Order Number: 452199

Order Date: 6/5/2013

Customer Name: LL's Catering
Phone: (302) 283-2398

Contact Person: Lauren Logan
Phone: (302) 824-7934 (cellular)

Reference: Earl Wedding

Delivery Location: St. Mark's Church, 281 Bell St., Wilmington, DE 19801

Delivery Date: 7/27/2013
Delivery Window: 2 pm - 4 pm

Pick-Up Date: 7/27/2013
Pick-Up Window: 11 pm - 12 am

	Ordered	Unit	Total Price
FLATWARE:			
Contemporary Style Tea Spoon	20	0.50	$10.00
Standard Serving Fork Ultra	5	2.00	$10.00
Standard Serving Spoon Ultra	20	2.00	$40.00
FLATWARE SUBTOTAL:			$60.00
SERVICE ITEMS:			
Coffee Brewer 36 Cup	4	14.00	56.00
Pitcher Glass	4	5.00	80.00
SERVICE ITEMS SUBTOTAL:			$136.00
LINENS:			
Lime 120" Tablecloth Round	11	15.00	$165.00
Orange 120" Tablecloth Round	11	15.00	$165.00
Dark Blue 60" Tablecloth Rectangular	10	20.00	$200.00
LINENS SUBTOTAL:			$530.00
DELIVERY CHARGE:	1	35.00	35.00
DELIVERY SUBTOTAL:			$35.00

Sample of an order receipt from the rental company

GROSS RENTAL	$726.00
DISCOUNT	($72.60)
SUBTOTAL	$653.40
SALES TAX	$40.84
DELIVERY CHARGE	$35.00
TOTAL DUE	$729.24

PAPER PRODUCTS

Paper products give rise to the same issues and pricing options as bar, beverages, and rentals. You will need to decide the quantities and styles needed, whether you will handle purchasing them for your client, and what you will charge if you acquire them. Some clients will want to obtain the paper products themselves; if so, due to the complexity of selecting paper products, you need to be especially clear when telling your client what they'll need.

Complex, you say? How complex can paper products be? Assessing the paper product requirements for an event is in fact trickier than it may initially seem. Consider the pacing of the event: if a buffet is open for hours, people will likely return multiple times, and they'll often take a new plate at each visit. Consider the set-up: will there be assigned seating, making it more likely for people to keep track of their plates, or will guests be mulling about, often depositing a plate or cup somewhere and forgetting it? Also consider the style of the food, as well as the overall style of the event. Will you use small plates in an attempt to keep small portions of expensive dishes from looking skimpy? So many considerations!

Many parties will use both paper products and china. It is important that you systematically determine exactly what you will need of each. Thoroughly review your menu, item by item, and visualize what takes paper, what takes china, etc. Don't forget toothpicks, skewers, cocktail napkins, etc. Unfortunately, with so many different products, it is easy to miss something. You may be thinking about serving a dessert item and forget about the cups for the coffee service, even if it's right there on the menu with your Bananas Foster.

DÉCOR AND DESIGN

When I originally created Miss Jeanies, I didn't realize that I had founded a catering company. Remember the teapots for my first job? The trays, lace, and fabrics I pulled together for that tea party I "catered"? From the beginning, my offering was more than just food: it was the whole food experience. And just as I created a catering company without realizing it, it was with a similar subconsciousness that I eventually developed a Décor and Design department at Miss Jeanies. I just started collecting unique items from yard sales, the Christmas Tree Shop, and almost every fabric store around Boston. Six years into Miss Jeanies, I found myself catering a local school auction with the theme "Everything Goes Roses," and I worked closely with the person heading décor for the PTO to create the event. She and I shared lots of ideas. We were clearly on the same creative wavelength. Not long after, I hired her to create the Décor and Design department at Miss Jeanies, whcih added an amazing dimension to our food.

Recall how one of the goals of your first meeting with your client was to find a hook that could tie together the entire event. **The specificity or concreteness of the hook will determine how tightly the décor needs to correlate**. For example, if you and your client decided upon a rather literal hook, such as "Parisian Café" then you'll almost automatically have some ideas of what the décor should include. Note that with this sort of event, décor can extend beyond decorating just the buffet tables and guest tables. It may mean decorating an entire room and ordering accessories that create an environment.

With more subtle hooks, or hooks that focus on what food will be served, you'll need to give further thought to how the design and décor can bring out the hook. On one hand, the task is easier, because you have more options. If the hook is "simple sophistication," for example, then you can choose from endless simple and sophisticated design schemes: black-and-white framed photos on the tables, or bowls of floating candles. On the other hand, it can be challenging to find ways to represent certain hooks through décor choices. Let's say you're catering a graduation party and the decided theme is "celebration." There's going to be lots of drinking, dancing, and a menu full of fun food. How does "celebration" translate into décor selections? It doesn't translate, not directly at least, so this is when you have to inquire further into

---

Ideas for....

One-Size-Fits-All Decor

Rather than coordinating design and décor based on food and ambiance of each individual event, you may want to settle upon a look or a brand that clients can count on when they hire you, Your standard offering could be simple-contemporary: elegant silver platters and starched white cloths. Or you may want to be more versatile and colorful in your presentation—funky and unconventional serving pieces, like sundaes in martini glasses. The possibilities are endless.

---

what your client wants. Are there certain colors they prefer? Would they like centerpieces that the guests can take home with them? Do they want to use consumables, like food and flowers, as décor? With enough information, you'll be able to come up with a decor plan that will please your client.

INVITATIONS

Invitations play an important role in any event. Whether elegantly expensive or creatively economical, they help create energy and provide information essential to helping make a party a rousing success.

More often than not, your client will have already completed their invitations before hiring you, yet I still recommend having referrals for several invitation vendors on hand. I even think you would do well to introduce yourself to any invitation vendors in your area ahead of time, as they will often see a potential client before you do and can thus be a great referral source. Establish a relationship with them by visiting their store with your business card. You might want to bring a gift as well—a nicely decorated basket of scones or a Mason jar of delicious soup will give them a good feeling about your business.

If you do work with the client on the invitation, I recommend advising them that guests will want to know what to expect regarding food. The guests will often want to eat accordingly before they arrive at an evnet. An invitation featuring an overly-explicit description of the menu can be tacky, as though the food needs to be advertised to get people to attend the event. Try instead to incorporate subtle hints of the menu into the invitation. For example, instead of titling an invite "Barbara's 50th Birthday Party," title it "Barbara's 50th Birthday Brunch." Simple as that. For an all-dessert party, you could write something like "Come Satisfy Your Sweet Tooth at Barbara's."

There's an exception to the rule that an invitation shouldn't state the planned menu outright. If the event is a formal, sit-down meal, the RSVP cards may include a line for Entrée Selection. Of course, for this to work, the entrées have to be planned before the invitations go out. Providing guests with a choice of entrée selection is more costly than a single entree, but for some clients it's a good use of money.

THE FAVOR OF A REPLY IS REQUESTED BY JUNE 1

_____

_____ ACCEPT WITH PLEASURE
_____ DECLINE WITH REGRET

PLEASE INITIAL AN ENTREE CHOICE FOR EACH GUEST

_____ HERB GRILLED FILET MIGNON
_____ SAFFRON BUTTER CRACKED LOBSTER
_____ PORTOBELLO MUSHROOM RAVIOLI

Not only should an invitation hint at the food, but it should make the overall style of the event known. This will give guests an idea of what to wear. For example, I recently catered an evening party with a menu that include Bacon, Egg, and Cheese sandwiches, home fries, and other diner fare. The client's wish was for guests to show up in party dresses, not jeans. On her invitation, she described the party as a "Dressy Diner", thus clueing the guests in on the food and attire for the evening. A description like "upscale BBQ" works similarly: guests know to dress for a fancier take on down-home food. You can really amp up the energy of a party well ahead of time by using the invitation to offer hints about the food, as well as the style, of the event.

PHOTOGRAPHER / VIDEOGRAPHER

I generally like clients to choose their own photographer as they have their own aesthetic sense to satisfy. And lucky for me, I have found that most clients will in fact handle this themselves. However, if you do end up arranging a photographer or videographer for the client, keep in mind that these services vary greatly in pricing. The more you know about the market, the better able you'll be to find an appropriate price for your client. Don't forget that you're allowed to collect an "upcharge' on the photographer's or videographer's fees.

It is always important to let the photographer know who or what to focus upon. I remember at a party I had for my son, I failed to be specific about the photos I wanted and ended up with hardly any pictures of my son or our family, and a multitude of pictures of a young, attractive guest! I would have assumed a photographer would know to take pictures of the honoree and family. Guess I was wrong.

MUSIC

Music can impact an event almost as much as the food menu, décor, design, and presentation. You will find that many clients choose DJs rather than live bands, so be prepared with referrals for good ones you have heard. I have found DJ costs to be the part of the event planning business where prices vary the most. This may come as a surprise to your client, so encourage them to do their homework in scouting out at DJ. Ideally, they may even attend an event to watch a potential hire. As a side note, you will find that DJs frequently charge for "give-away products" such as hats, sunglasses, and necklaces, and you should let your client know there are vendors where they can purchase these items themselves, saving costs.

Some clients do prefer a live band to a DJ. Although many clients already know what band they want or where to find a band, it is wise that you again have a referral list of a range of musicians in case they don't. If you do end up choosing the band, it is important to know specifically what type of band your client may want for their event, as there are many different types available.

It will be up to you to be sure the voltage and plugs at the event site are adequate for the musicians' needs more than likely, you will be the only one to visit the site ahead of time. As always, planning ahead will help you avoid stress on the day of the event!

When working with musicians or a DJ, you will need to go over the schedule of the event and choreograph any relevant details. Talk about whether there will be dancing throughout the evening without a break for dinner, or a dinner break during which soft music is played, etc. Beware that some entertainers are quite opinionated about how the event should run. It takes an open dialogue between the caterer, the musician, and the client to schedule a great event.

Some clients will want to use a digital music player such as an iPod as their music source. This is a much easier (and cheaper) method than using a band or DJ. They will create playlists ahead of time and ask that you or one of your staff turn it on at a particular moment. It will fall upon you to see whether the event site has a speaker system to which you can connect the client's iPod or laptop. A high-quality sound dock is another item you could personally purchase and offer to rent to clients for a small fee, especially if you cater a lot of events at homes.

ADDITIONAL ENTERTAINMENT

Clients may want you to help them find special entertainment for their party, such as magicians, fortune-tellers, T-shirt designers, or temporary-tattoo artists. You'd be surprised by the ever-changing ideas about strategies and products to entertain guests. Photo booths, for example, are hot at the moment. I suggest doing a Google search every several months to see what's happening in the party entertainment field and keep it in mind when meeting with your clients.

VALET SERVICES

Helping arrange valet services, or hired parking, can be as quick as making a phone call. Just make sure to check the references of a business or group of individuals to be sure they are reputable. Prices tend to be competitive but check out a few for your client.

So, do you want to add event planning to your company's repertoire? Now that you are aware of event planning services and the work that goes into providing them, you can decide on the route you want to take. Don't force it. The client will feel it. Far better you say "no thank you" to event planning and a huge thank you for the classic catering part!!

CHAPTER NINE
Preparing Your Policy Sheet

MAKING SURE THAT YOUR FINE PRINT IS CLEAR
AND SPECIFIC WILL GO A LONG WAY TOWARD
SAVING YOU FROM ENDLESS AGGRAVATION.

. . . .

You've figured out your pricing. Now it's time to put together the
final package for your client. This proposal packet should include:

♦ Cover Letter
♦ Business Card
♦ Proposed Menu
♦ Proposed Budget
♦ Policy Sheet

We've gone over how to produce a business card, menu, and budget.
The cover letter need only include a few sentences outlining what you've
included in the packet and what the next step is (i.e. you look forward
to hearing from this prospective client, or you will follow-up with them
by a certain time).

We'll now take a look at the Policy Sheet. A Policy Sheet communicates information about your business in an official tone. It gives your
client certainty that you are in control of your business. Your Policy
Sheet will help you manage difficult clients as well as issues or conflicts
that may come your way.

Determining what you want to include in your Policy Sheet can take
years of practice. It certainly took me a long time to figure out what
policies would protect my business yet be fair to my clients. This chapter will give you a head start by describing the policies that compose my
policy sheet, but eventually you should modify them to fit your needs.
Based on the specific nature of your business, some of these may not be
applicable, or you may need additional policies. Ready to go?

FINANCIAL POLICIES

Deposits

Your policy sheet should state that once the client accepts your proposed menu and budget, they must give you a deposit to hold the date of the event. I have found that putting down a deposit actually makes clients feel good. They are relieved to have hired a caterer, and the deposit makes them feel they can relax until closer to their occasion. You will be taking care of things.

As there is no industry standard on deposit amounts and/or timing, you can determine what you'd like for a deposit. You may want to collect 50% upfront, 30% more the week of the job and 20% the day of the event. Or you may want to collect 20% upfront, 70% the week before the event and collect the final 10% the week following it.

While photographers, bands, bartenders and other event vendors frequently collect the balance of their deposit at the event, I prefer not to do this. It has always struck me as more respectful of the client's special day to not have the exchange of money associated with my services. I prefer to collect the balance due in the days following the event. This could leave me open to a possible collection problem, but it rarely has. Only once did this happen: I catered a Bar Mitzvah for a couple in the process of a divorce, who later used each other as an excuse not to pay the balance despite being thrilled with our services!

The Bottom Line? **Whichever way you decide to manage the deposit, put your guidelines in writing on your policy sheet.** I have found that clients are generally flexible with however I handle it.

Cancellations

In the beginning of setting up your business, you may find it hard to imagine needing a cancellation policy. In effect, a cancellation policy protects your time. If by chance another person calls you for the same date, you may refuse the second job in order to do an outstanding job for your first client. If the first client changes their mind because they hear about a cheaper caterer or because they decide to go on a vacation to celebrate their anniversary rather than hosting a party, you've lost the second client—the money and business goodwill.

I think it's useful to have a cancellation policy in place on your initial policy sheet. You can always "make an exception" under special circumstances. For example if you truly believe a wedding was cancelled due to a broken engagement and you didn't turn away another job while holding that date, you could decide to refund the deposit. Just let this be your decision to do, not the client.

You can have an "all or nothing policy" that no matter when the client cancels, the client will lose their deposit, albeit if the cancellation occurs the day after they give you the deposit or a week before the job. Or your policy could be that if a client cancels before the week of the job, you'll return 50% of their deposit, but if they cancel the week of the job, you won't return any of it. One thing for sure, you need to be compensated for any items you've purchased for the job if it is cancelled. Imagine you've wisely purchased shrimp on sale two weeks before the party for a "Shrimp in Many Ways" buffet and freeze them. You don't want to be left with 40 pounds of shrimp with no jobs in sight with shrimp on their menu! You also need to be compensated for the time you put into the job, whether it took the form of meeting with the client, drafting a menu, or making arrangements with vendors.

> **Things to Consider...**
>
> ## When to Cash a Check
>
> When you collect a deposit from the client, you have the choice of cashing that check right away or holding onto it until the job gets closer. If you need the money up-front, it's acceptable to cash the client's check in advance of the job. You likely won't be putting that money directly toward their event; instead, you'll siphon the funds to where you need them at present moment. Just keep in mind your deposit return policy. If you state that you'll return 50% of a client's deposit if they cancel with two weeks notice, they're going to expect that money back the second they call off the event; if you've gone out and spent their whole deposit on a new stove, you may end up in trouble.

Then there is a "rain" or "natural disaster" cancellation clause. Believe it or not, depending upon where you live, hurricanes can be a possible cause for cancellation. An outdoor party with no rain plan can eventuate in a cancelled party. As sympathetic as you may be for your client, you are running a business and you may want to protect yourself against Mother Nature. You could offer a "rain date" policy wherein you reschedule the event for the client if possible. Yet, you don't have to be extra flexible. Watching the weather the week of a party and not knowing whether to go ahead and purchase your products can be nerve wracking.

So what should you charge for a party cancelled due to weather, elements beyond a client's control? The whole deposit or 90% of your proposed price? Perhaps 100% of your proposed price and an offer of a small dinner party for free?

Cost of Event Staff

Your policy sheet needs to spell out the details about how you will charge for event staff. Your client should know they will be charged from the time your staff comes to your "commissary" to load up the job until the time staff members return after the party to unload the job. Clients frequently do not realize that these behind-the-scenes operations are part of staffing a party. They just visualize staff in the kitchen at the party and serving on the floor.

It is also important to give the client the agreed upon "end time" for event staff. The client must know she will be charged more for her staff if a party goes longer than anticipated. You can specify hourly rates per each staff member, i.e. "extra 20 dollars per hour per staff member working after 11:30 PM" or the cost for all staff for each additional hour, i.e. "an extra 200 dollars per half hour the party extends after11:30 PM, .regardless of how many staff members remain."

Things to Consider...

The Ideal Length of a Staff Member's Shift

Many catering companies require a minimum shift length per staff member at an event, but I never have. Typically, the nature of a party will ensure a 4-5 hour shift for my staff.; quick cocktail parties, brunches, or "continuation parties" are exceptions you may need to address.

One advantage of not having a minimm shift length for staff memebrs is that you can be more precise in using the right amount of staff for the scenario of the party. For example, a party may commence with lots of appetizer stations, so you have to hire a large number of staff to work the first two hours of the party. Then, once the party shifts into a buffet, a handful of those staff members can head home.

Sales Tax

Laws regarding catering and sales tax vary by state. In Ohio, for instance, the law specifies that a caterer does not need to collect sales tax when food is sold for consumption off-the-premises; by this standard, a full-service off-premise caterer would not have to tax their food, as their food is consumed somewhere other than at the site of production. Think that's tricky? It gets worse. An Ohio caterer *does* have to tax products such as beverages and rentals. Bottom line: become an expert on the sales tax requirements in your state, and be sure to explain these to your client. Just as consumers are accustomed to paying sales tax on items they purchase in stores, a client will understand their obligation to pay you sales tax on top of your proposed price.

Gratuities

Almost every client asks whether there is a required gratuity, i.e. whether they should tip the staff. Large catering companies automatically include a required gratuity for their staff, just as restaurants will often do for large parties. Industry standard for this gratutity is about 20% above staff charge.

I have always made certain my staff was paid significantly higher than industry standard. Hence, my policy was to welcome, but not to require, gratuity. I would discuss this with the client at our first meeting, explaining "Gratuity is not required, but certainly my staff always appreciates receiving a gratuity." Typically, clients do then offer gracious, tips for my staff, which are very well-appreciated.

Guest Numbers

There are multiple things that need to be laid out when writing your Guest Numbers policy. First of all, you will need to decide the date on which the client must confirm the number of guests attending. This might vary based on the specific of the event; for instance, if you do not need to provide numbers to any outside vendors, you may decide on a date just a few weeks in advance of the event.

Next, you may want to establish a minimum charge per event, based on event type. Guest numbers change, and typically the number of guests falls beneath the client's initial prediction. If a client tells you they expect to have 100 guests at an event, you are going to craft your menu and budget with that number in mind (if you've forgotten that food and labor costs are not directly proportional to the number of guests, flip back to page 84). If that number later drops to 70 confirmed guests, you're going to be in trouble. Even if you can produce the menu with a reduced budget, you may have been counting upon making a certain profit from this job. If you had set a minimum price for a job, then no matter what, you would still be guaranteed that amount of profit.

What to do if the guests number exceed the original prediction? There are several options. You could still charge your established price per guest, or you could be generous and reduce the per person amount for the additional guests only. It's up to you as to what you feel comfortable in charging. Figure out a way to trade off a financial plus for you with client goodwill.

LEFTOVERS

Believe it or not, this can be a tricky subject. Although you'd think it would be a matter of whether to leave leftovers for your client or not, it's more than that.

The standard policy in the catering industry is that **you are only required to provide the food neccessary to satisfy the number of committed guests.** Anything in excess of serving the guests is the property of the caterer. At Miss Jeanies our policy is that all food that we have prepared for the event belongs to the client. However, any un-prepared and uncooked items, like produce, are Miss Jeanies property. How does this pan out? Let's look at a couple scenarios.

	BACK TO YOUR COMMISSARY	GIVE TO YOUR CLIENT
Example: Omelettes You bring ten dozen eggs for an omelette bar, but only go through eight dozen. You also are left with an unopened package of smoked salmon, half a wheel of asiago cheese, and a quart of chopped tomatoes.	The two dozen eggs are yours to keep. You agreed to provide each guest with as many omelettes as they desired; this is different from selling the client a set number of eggs.	The client probably won't have much use for the tomatoes, which will spoil quickly. But they might appreciate a few pieces of smoked salmon or a nice wedge of cheese.
Example: Pizza You bring pizza crusts to a job and cook five pizzas on site. One of the pizzas is placed on the buffet but barely touched, and one cooked pizza remains in the kitchen. You're also left with two unused pizza crusts.	The two unused crusts are without question yours to keep. As for the pizza that you cooked but didn't put out, it's your call. Does it count as prepared food or not?	The pizza that was placed on the buffet belongs to the client. It's open to interpretation whether the pizza that got cooked but never left the kitchen belongs to them as well.

Clients can go either way on leftovers. Some don't like too many leftovers. They perceive them as a waste of food, or as a signal that they could have gotten away with a smaller budget. At the other end of the spectrum, some clients want to keep each and every last piece of food. I've had clients who keep a keen eye on the buffet table throughout the party, trying to gauge the prognosis for their leftovers.

It is next to impossible to predict the exact amount of food that a party will require. Even after all my years of catering, I remain amazed at how the same demographic group will eat differently at two different events two weeks in a row! Therefore I always make certain that when shopping (see Chapter 14), I get the supplies needed to make more than enough of each item on the menu. Needless to say, making more than enough of each item on the menu virtually guarantees leftovers! The loss of client goodwill resulting from running out of food would be a far worse blow to my business.

> Decide your own leftover policy. I believe it is your **obligation** as the caterer to make certain that the client gets the food you agreed to provide, not anything more.

When discussing your leftover policy with your client, explain that it is next to impossible to calculate exact amounts and there will nearly always be leftovers. Tell them that the alternative is running out of certain menu items. Ask them about their comfort level with this—I have found very few clients are comfortable with running out of food. You should also ask your client how they would like their leftovers packaged, whether in Ziploc bags or in aluminum catering pans.

It is good to put aside a few items from each course to leave as a sampling for the client. Frequently, they are so busy socializing, they don't have time to taste the food at their own party! Be sure to consider which items will hold up over time so that the client can fully appreciate the quality of your work. Clients greatly appreciate this gesture. Also tell your client that you will only be giving her food items that you deem safe to take home, according to Serve Safe standards. Some caterers actually don't want to take the risk of sending home food with clients, for fear of potential legal issues. For example, if food leaves a party in safe condition, then is mishandled and eaten at a later time, and someone gets sick, the caterer is potentially liable. You will need to figure out your comfort levels around this and determine your policy accordingly.

OTHER POLICIES

Trash Removal

Believe it or not, trash is an ongoing issue at every job. Many caterers charge a separate line item amount just for removal. You'd be amazed how much there is to dispose of at the end of a party. Where does it go? You can use your trash cans at your own home or rent a dumpster at your commissary. Sometimes facilities will allow you to use their dumpster for free, while some will charge a trash fee (which you will then want to pass on to your client). Trash removal should not be an expense absorbed by your business.

Rentals and Liquor Pick-Up

Who is responsible for rental, liquor and other vendor pick-ups after the party is over? It is easy for both the client and the caterer to neglect these. You may get such a sense of relief after producing a successful party that, once you know you've pulled it off, you let go and forget to take care of the followup duties. Therefore, determine ahead of time whether you or the client will take responsibility for rental returns and vendor pickups. If the event is at the client's house (or office, etc.), it's usually better to schedule pickups for the day after the event.

Be explicit with your client about the possibility of rental and vendor costs changing. For example, if a party runs over, and the rental company arrives at the site to find that you're unready to return all their items, they'll likely charge you an additional fee. Make sure the client knows that these sort of charges are a possibility, and that they will be responsible should such charges occur.

Tastings

Many large catering companies, and even some small ones, offer a "tasting" of menu items for clients. However, rarely have clients requested it in the many years I have run Miss Jeanies, and I have never actually needed to provide one.

For a small catering business, preparing tasting is practically as much work as catering an entire party. You would need to go through every shopping and cooking step as you would for the actual event. Even if you charged for the time and products required for a tasting, it becomes a costly and difficult business practice. Tastings can leave a catering company open to unnecessary headaches, wasting needless time, energy, and resources.

That being said, I do appreciate that clients want to taste what they are choosing to serve their guests. Once, I even contemplated delivering food for clients to try as a "tasting alternative." However, I continued to believe this experience does not in any way capture the true essence of our food. The same food will be experienced far differently at a party than at a private tasting. Once again, there is a gestalt of senses coming together at a party that is impossible to create at a private tasting.

The bottom line is that **every chef and every item will produce a slightly different eating experience every time.** There is the risk that the food at a tasting might taste differently to the client at the party. I have even heard of clients that didn't like the food at tastings, demanding another tasting, and then another, until they were satisfied. In essence, they had five dinner parties before their actual event!

Instead of a tasting, I encourage clients to speak with someone familiar with Miss Jeanies to get an idea about our food and presentations. Previous clients, as well as guests who have attended our events, are great sources of information. Additionally, I will tell clients that I am happy to explain the ingredients that go into a particular recipe. Ultimately, clients are content with these alternative reassurances.

Your experience may vary, and you may even enjoy the process of satisfying clients with tastings of particular items and recipes. As always, follow your head and your heart on this.

Although you can't ALWAYS steer clear of conflict with your client, a thorough and clear policy sheet helps keep it to a minimum.

BEYOND THE POLICY SHEET: THE LEGAL CONTRACT

A Legal Contract sounds so serious, doesn't it? I don't actually use one regularly. I give my clients the comprehensive proposal packet and policy sheet, and I take their deposit: this functions as my contract. However, I do have a legal contract available should a particular client request it. I also have drafted a separate "Save the Date" deposit contract. This would be used, for instance, when there's no budget or menu yet, just a wedding two years in the future.

If you do decide to put together a legal contract, then I suggest you have a lawyer draft one for you to ensure you are aware of the legal issues involved with catering an event (See Page 172 for more). Your aim is to protect your new business from loss, and it's best to use a pro to make sure this is done right.

SIGNED, SEALED, DELIVERED.

You've pulled together all the components of your proposal, and it hasn't been easy. Check it one last time, go over your numbers, and then get it to your client. After you drop that envelope in the mailbox or hit send on the computer, give yourself a moment to feel proud of what you've achieved.

So, what's next?

Now is a good time to switch gears and return to the more creative side of things. Maybe go back to looking through some food magazines and cookbooks or perhaps explore local stores for fun items you can use in your event presentations. Get rejuvenated and reinspired. Continue to dream and imagine your events. You're about to step foot into your kitchen!

RECIPE REQUIREMENT: Something that
Reheats Well

I adore serving paninis at cocktail parties. The sky's the limit on the combinations of fillings that can be made into a delicious grilled sandwich. After running many tests, I found that when necessary, one can go ahead and do the first round of panini grilling 2 days ahead *without compromising the quality of the food.* Then, right before serving, reheat the paninis in a panini press or in an oven. You may just want to rebaste with a little extra butter.

Pumpkin, Brie, and Shortbread Paninis

INGREDIENTS:
Bread (almost anything will work, but it should sliced medium-thick so it
        can stand up to melting ingredients. Ciabatta is a good choice.)
Pumpkin jam
Brie
Almonds (can toast or spice as you wish)
Box of Walker's shortbread cookies or another brand, crushed

Cut up and mix all ingredients together in a bowl. Make sure your pumpkin jam provides enough moisture.

Baste outside of bread lightly with butter, then spread mixture on inside. Press sandwiches in a panini press*

Let cool down on a sheet pan/parchment paper. Do not stack sandwiches, and do not cut them.

Put away in refrigerator, being careful to keep sandwiches separate.

At party, reheat sandwiches. If you have the press on site, it can be used for the reheating; if not, heat paninis on trays in the oven. After reheating, cut and serve.

*Here's a tip. If you don't have a panini press, you can grill your sandwiches by placing on a ridged pan or griddle and then placing a heavy object, such as another skittle or a empty tea kettle, on top. DIY sandwich press!

CHAPTER TEN
Setting Up Your Kitchen

YOU'RE HIRED. NOW WHAT DO YOU DO UNTIL THE WEEK OF YOUR JOB? GET YOUR KITCHEN AND EQUIPMENT ORGANIZED AND READY.

. . . .

It is rare for anyone starting out to have a beautifully-configured kitchen with walk in refrigerators, endless counter space and the latest pots and pans and equipment. Unless you have a private income, you will probably not have the luxury of cooking in a state-of-the-art commercial kitchen. Neither did I. As a matter of fact, rarely have any successful caterers started their businesses in a grand space.

You can start with your existing equipment and space. One of the most appealing aspects of the business is that you don't need to purchase very much equipment to begin catering.

To begin, look at what you already own. For my first event, the 40th birthday celebration featuring an afternoon tea, I only had a stove with four burners, one of which was not working. You know what? It was a useful experience. I had to immediately learn to think about how to cook the entire menu with only three burners available. It was a crash course in the art of sequencing! My first "culinary kitchen" was indeed basic. I still enjoy catering in non-complicated cooking settings.

A large aspect of professional cooking is about making do with what you have. **It is not about the magnitude or magnificence of the equipment, but about figuring out how to maximize the usage of the equipment available to you**. At a catering job, you could find yourself in a kitchen far less efficient than your own. Or you could be working a job in a luxury kitchen with the newest appliances and gadgets. **Your challenge as a caterer is to figure out how to produce a menu no matter what the environment.**

KITCHEN EQUIPMENT

Refrigerator and Stove

Obviously the two critical appliances you will need for the core of your catering business are a **refrigerator** and **stove**. Whether it's a commercial Viking with eight burners, a grill with a hood, or a four-burner gas stove with a single oven rack, you can make it work. Sure, it may take you twice as long to produce four dozen white chocolate chip scones if you're using a small oven, but maybe you can take advantage of that extra baking time to get your spinach and feta salad ready or do a load of dishes.

A large refrigerator is good, but it's even better to have a second one to store additional items. I truly believe that it is more important to invest in a second refrigerator than a second stove. You will need it. I definitely don't recommend using a friend or family member's refrigerator as secondary cold storage space. Someone else may accidentally leave the door open, or a thunderstorm may temporarily cause a power outage, or a hungry child may even decide to stick an unwashed finger in your product. Whatever becomes of the food is your responsibility.

> You are responsible for the safety of the food that you serve, and you are not in control of food that is out of your sight. Always keep your food somewhere where you can monitor it.

You should always closely monitor the temperature of your refrigerator. I cannot overly stress the importance of keeping it below 41 degrees Fahrenheit at all times. To ensure appropriate heating and cooling, you will need a commercial thermometer. Buy at least two; they are inexpensive. Put them at different locations in your refrigerator to monitor possible fluctuating temperatures. You cannot afford to have a guest get sick thanks to food that was spoiled by fluctuating refrigerator temperatures. Not only would you feel terrible about this, but your business would come to an abrupt halt.

It is nice to have a commercial-size freezer, but it's not a necessity. For the most part, catering demands the use of food that's fresh, not frozen. However, it is helpful to have freezer space. For example, you find a wonderful sale on chicken breasts for an upcoming event, and you can purchase 20 pounds ahead of time and freeze them. Or, certain desserts such as chocolate mousse freeze beautifully, reducing last minute stress by making them a day or so ahead of an event

Pots and Pans

Whatever you have for pots and pans, my guess is that those will work fine for you first few jobs. As time goes on, you may need to purchase specific pots for certain jobs. I have to admit that one of the best pots i ever owned was rather pricey. But I found it to be a one of a kind product, fabulous for cooking large batches of grains, rice, meats, and stews.

When you look into purchasing pots and pans, it's a good idea to check out restaurant supply houses first. The quality and weight of commercial pots and pans are noticeably different than many normal household items. These added features come in useful when producing large quantities of food. However, I certainly don't think you need to own the most expensive commercial products, at least not at the start. That said, if you currently own sheet pans which you purchased at a local supermarket or cooking store, I highly recommend you eventually shift to commercial grade ones. What's so special about commercial grade pans? They are more durable and maintain a more consistent level of heat.

When purchasing pans or pots, be sure to check their size to make sure they will fit into your oven. More importantly, check to be sure that they will fit into ovens at most event sites. Some high-end, renovated kitchens have ovens that only accommodate tiny sheet pans, which are far smaller than typical commercial sheet pans.

Over time you will determine the sizes of pots and pans with which you are most comfortable when cooking large quantities. Even when I am cooking rice for 200 people, I still choose to make 60 servings at a time. I prefer to not use the largest pot available. I find for some items, cooking in quantity can be tricky, so I'd rather use smaller pots and repeat the process several times rather than compromise the quality cooked in one huge pot. In Chapter 12, we'll talk more about cooking in large quantities.

be open

to new ideas and suggestions for improvement while simultaneously keeping a discerning eye. Ultimately, you make the final decisions for the equipment that will help to grow your business.

Cutting and Chopping Tools

A word of warning about kitchen utensils: stay out of high-end cooking stores! They are a dangerous place to be, for you will want every utensil you see. Colors, shapes, woods, and metals will all try to allure you. Don't let it happen! Ultimately, **you determine your own requirements for special cooking utensils**: Maybe you can't go without your mandolin, which is ideal for slicing foods many different thicknesses. I know if I had to pick one "bonus" utensil, I'd choose my microplane zester, which I use for zesting and grating products very finely. Overall, however, I keep my utensils to a minimum.

So what are the bare minimum requirements for utensils? In reality, all you really need are good knives and cutting boards, some quality large spoons, a grater and a whisk. With knives, chefs often choose the particular line and style they cherish and enjoy working with the most. I personally have only on rare occasion found a particular knife that I adored. Yet, if I had to choose one style it would be ceramic knives. They are light and agile.

> Remember: keep your knives sharpened. A dull knife wastes time and is hard on the wrists.

Have at least five cutting boards designated for categories such as vegetables and fruits, potatoes and breads, chicken, beef, and fish. Categorizing cutting boards provides an additional measure of safety in preventing cross contamination of your products. A lightweight plastic cutting board works just as well as a wooden one

Goodbye, Garlic Press

I have to confess, I adore garlic in my food. Almost all of my sauces and dishes for my savories contain at least one pod of garlic. Garlic doesn't need to dominate a dish; in fact, I believe that behind the scenes it makes food dance. When I first began catering, I could not have done without my Garlic Press. I used it constantly. It was easy and efficient. I did not even have to peel the garlic. I could whip through many heads of garlic in no time. However, once I discovered that big bottles of already peeled garlic were commercially available, I was overjoyed. What a joy to start a day of cooking by pureeing several pods of garlic in my food processor! Alas, my best sous chef, the garlic press, was retired.

from a high-end cooking store. In fact, I recommend you replace your cutting boards frequently for cleanliness reasons; as such, it is advantageous to buy less costly ones.

I would not cook and cater without a food processor. It is a necessity. It will save you hours of work and increase your efficiency. You will eventually learn what steps can or cannot be sped up without compromising the quality of your food. Over time, I've learned just how long to "pulse" certain foods or when to use the "puree" setting. I've learned which foods lose their integrity in the food processor and which blend into delicious combinations and concoctions. That said, if you do not currently have a food processor and are not in the habit of cooking with one, you certainly do not have to run out and buy one.

Storage and Labeling Supplies

Having adequate and efficient storage containers will make your catering life a whole lot easier. This may sound insignificant, but I consider it a core ingredient in your success. Not having the right containers can slow down your production significantly and can result in inadequately stored food. I suggest purchasing plastic pint and quart containers and tops at a restaurant supply store or on the internet. You can supplement these with recycled jars and plastic containers from previously purchased products. However, your local health department may require that you use commercial-grade food safe storage containers.

Disposable alumnimum containers with lids are the mainstay of a caterer's kitchen. These too can be purchased at restaurant supply stores or found on the internet. You will eventually need them in various sizes. They, at first, will seem like an expense you would like to do without, but you will grow to appreciate their reliability in storing your finished product. Plastic baggies or Ziplocs will also become your best friends.

Commercial-size rolls of aluminum foil and plastic wrap are fabulous. They will save you money in the long run and certainly save many trips to the store. They also guarantees secure, tighter packaging as well as storage. Parchment paper is another thing I would never want to be without. It minimizes your chances of burning what you are baking. You never have to soak and scrape your sheet pans. It is wise to buy parchment paper in large quantities as it will be needed time and time again.

You will need a good labeling system. This can be as low tech as a roll of masking tape and a permanent marker or as complex as color-coded, computer-made labels. At first, labeling your items will be simple as you will more than likely be the one doing the majority of the cooking, delivering, setting up, and serving your food. Yet, the second you add in a second person or multiple jobs, you'll need a labeling system to keep track of everything. Prevent mistakes and avoid frustration. Labeling your food carefully can make the difference in matching the correct sauce with the correct menu item, getting the right food to the right event, and more.

Serving Pieces

You will hopefully have fun acquiring your serving dishes. Continuously build your collection! Always be on the look out for a particularly good price on a great salad bowl or serving platter and treat yourself to it. It won't go to waste. Remember that the less heavy and less fragile it is the better. And, you definitely don't have to go high end. Go to yard sales and flea markets as well as traditional shops.

Over time, **the style of your serving pieces will evolve to express your brand.** Don't be concerned if you are not sure of your brand as yet. It is a process that will develop along your way. For me, I adore finding unique items for presentation that continue to evolve my brand. I find that the hunt for that one unusual bowl or platter is a great way re-engage and re-invigorate my catering business.

KITCHEN DESIGN:
MAXIMIZING ORGANIZATION AND FUNCTIONALITY

Many textbooks say, "The design and function of your catering kitchen is key to the success of your catering business." I disagree. It may make cooking a little easier, perhaps save a little labor time, but I certainly do not think there is any one way to set up for success in your kitchen. I believe you will be able to succeed in whatever kitchen, design flow, and equipment you come across.

Ideally, it is best to cook in a commercial kitchen. Believe it or not, you can find opportunities in your own community. Churches, schools, small restaurants, community centers, and even other catering companies may have kitchen space you could rent or sublet. You may find that these facilities are looking for ways to supplement their expenses and would be delighted to share their space with you. Since these sites are already health department approved, you may easily begin your catering business in them without having to go through necessary legitimizing procedures.

If you *do* decide to open your own commercial space at any point in your catering business, you will encounter many requirements regarding the equipment you must own and the processes you must follow. At first I assumed that going through these rigors would totally overwhelm me. I had no idea what I was doing. All I had heard were horror stories of health departments making it difficult to establish a catering business. Truthfully, it was not a difficult experience. There are steps you must take, requirements and regulations for you to follow, but if you take them seriously, all will go well. I found the health department receptive and helpful. Yes, there were fire marshals, plumbers, inspectors, electricians, building departments, and all kinds of city government departments involved. But taken one step at a time, it was very manageable.

> **The Future of Catering...**
>
> *Incubators*
>
> There are a growing number of places called "incubators" or licensed health department spaces where start-up food businesses can rent space by the hour or by the month to produce and store their food. If you decide to explore this option, I recommend you investigate the requirements of the health department in your town.

Setting Up a Commercial Kitchen

Let me give you a brief rundown of some of the requirements and steps of setting up a commercial kitchen. It is good to know what goes into a safe, efficient kitchen for cooking professionally.

First of all, health departments require a "plan drawing". This typically includes a kitchen configuration which must feature a 3 bay sink, a hand washing sink, and a mop sink. It also includes a refrigerator, a stove, a hood, work tables made out of the proper metal, a freezer, a loading area, proper electrical outlets, lighting and ventilation. Some health departments require floor drains in order that floors can be hosed down. Each health department has its own regulations for the standards and requirements of each of these components.

Once the health department approves your plan drawing for your kitchen, you will need a building permit from the building department. You must have this before you can begin any construction of a new kitchen or remodeling of an existing one.

The best way to configure a kitchen is to think about an efficient and safe layout. Separate the hot food production and prep areas from the cold food ones. Make sure that clean-up areas for pots and other equipment don't interfere with production. Ideally, include a storage space near the delivery and loading area for easy access.

Clearly the heating, plumbing, ventilating, air conditioning and electrical systems must be in place and inspected before walls, floors, and ceilings can be closed up and painted. You will find that your building and health departments have specific requirements for electrical and plumbing set up. The electrical set up of your space is especially important. Make sure your wiring is updated and you have adequate power supply and access to prevent blowing out circuits at critical times. In the end, the Fire Marshal will check off on the safety of your electrical set-up.

Once your equipment is installed, your health department will conduct a final inspection of your space. Imagine the excitement when your first commercial kitchen is approved for business!

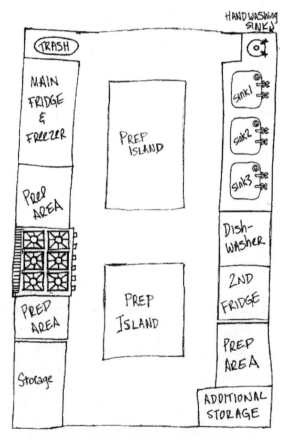

HERE'S A BASIC KITCHEN LAYOUT.
WHAT WOULD YOU ADD OR REDESIGN IF YOU COULD
CREATE YOUR OWN KITCHEN?

How to Work in Any Kitchen

It is critical to make sure your kitchen, commercial or not, is clean and easy to work in. Maximize your work surface space by eliminating clutter. Take a moment to look at what has accumulated on your countertops. Clean off and store the items used daily by your family. You are producing a professional product now! Over the years, I became an expert at transforming my home kitchen from a family kitchen to one that can accommodate cooking my menus. Think of it as a set design change in a play. After I was finished preparing my catering jobs, I would then change the set back to the "family set," and it always seemed to look a little more put-together than it did before I began!

Once you have cleared space, imagine cooking for your first job. For example, I always keep my food processor out; it has special status on my countertop and I use it in almost all my menus. However, I keep my heavy mixer, used mainly for whipping cream, under my counter (If you do a lot of baking, you probably make more frequent use of your heavy mixer! If so, keep it on the counter). Another way that I save space is by keeping my knives on a mounted magnetic bar instead of in a bulky countertop knife block.

While de-cluttering and maximizing your workspace, keep in mind how you want to set up your work areas, or "stations," for producing your jobs. Consider that the area around your stove will probably be your most-used surface, so clear as much space as possible. Have herbs, spices, and staples such as oil, vinegar, and cooking spray nearby for frequent use. Keep your main cooking utensils there too. If possible, hang your pots and pans and store your lids nearby. If you can't hang them above your stove, then be sure all pots, pans, and lids are organized underneath the counters. Don't forget the oven mitts! Keep them in a drawer close, but not too close, to your stove. You don't want anything made of fabric to catch on fire!

Your second most-used space will be near your food processor as this is a natural space for cutting and chopping. You will find it most efficient to have this space near your sink and to store cutting boards and knives here. Throw in colanders and small bowls to prep different foods, and you are ready to start producing!

If you plan to include baking in your catering business, you will need to create a baking area that is clear and sanitized for preparing baked goods and rolling out dough. Store your baking powder, flour, and other frequently used ingredients near this space.

It's a good idea to have easy access to your storage containers and packaging materials. Keep cleaning supplies near too, but remember to keep them safely away from where you are cooking. Also, try to think about minimizing hard-to-clean spaces such as between the stove and countertop where crumbs and spills can accumulate.

Having a system of organization for when you unload groceries for cooking saves worlds of time and frustration. It's worth the extra moment of thought. My organization system varies. Sometimes I organize the refrigerator, grouping together all dairy items, all vegetables, all meats, and so forth. Other times I group things by recipe. Regardless, it's important to place the ingredients you will be using first towards the front of your storage areas, and those you will need last at the back. If there are items that you will probably use more than once, place them within easy reach. Label all food and put it away in an organized manner.

ONCE ORGANIZED ....

IHave you noticed that after a half an hour or so in your kichen you enter a "zone" of cooking and production? It never ceases to amaze me. I can begin cooking my agenda for the day with self-consciousness, noticing every step I take. Recipes seem detailed and arduous. But sometime within the hour, I become aware that I have lost the moment-to-moment awareness of what I'm doing. I find myself "in the zone."

Once there, I can produce for hours and hours, moving from one task to the next, seeing the menu and subsequent agenda as long but doable. Before I know it, five or six hours have passed, but it seems

FOR ME, SUCH A SPACE IS A PORTAL TO *"The Zone."*

as though no time has passed at all. It is a great feeling to become one with the cooking. There is an ease and a sense of serenity.

Kitchen Sanitation

Next, let's address kitchen sanitation as it relates to organization and design. You're always going to have to do certain things to sanitize your kitchen; if you organize and design the space with that in mind, you'll be able to do these things better and more quickly.

Hand-washing is of major importance for your food safety, and should not be taken lightly. When possible, hands should be washed in a separate sink from where your food is being prepared. More and more it seems that hand-washing is considered the most effective means to prevent the spreading of germs and bacteria. We will explore further how to insure your food safety in Chapter 11.

Sanitize the sink you are using as you work. You will probably not have the luxury of the health department's three required sinks. My suggestion is to clear out your sink every time you finish working on a menu item, even if this takes up a few minutes of your time. This keeps your food safe and keeps you organized. Change your sponges frequently and make sure your rags are washed in washing machines on highest cycles. Use hot, soapy water, antibacterial cleaner, or diluted bleach for disinfecting your surface space. If you have a dishwasher, clear it out before you begin your day's cooking agenda. You will not want to stop to unload it once you are in motion.

If possible, designate an area of your kitchen where you will store items while they are cooling down before you put them in refrigeration or storage. This is where you'll be packaging cooked foods for storage, and you don't want any interactions with raw ingredients to occur. An inexpensive four or six foot folding rectangle table can be indispensable for this and other tasks.

Your refrigerator needs to be organized, cleared, and cleaned out frequently. When you complete a job, remove all leftovers before shopping for the next. Only keep dressings and sauces if you are 100% certain that no spoilage could have taken place. I have been extraordinarily cautious about saving leftovers and reusing items for the next job. The money I would save in re-using a product never seemed worth the potential risks and subsequent "what if" scenarios. I am sure some caterers are less cautious and trust their judgment more than I and save some money this way, but I'd rather be safe than sorry. Most likley olive oils, fresh produce, and seasonings that haven't interacted with other products can all be stored and reused. Non-mayonnaise vinaigrettes are certainly safe for a while. You will want to become an expert in "leftover safety" by taking ServSafe courses, talking to others in the catering field and by your collective experience.

It is very important not to overfill your refrigerator! Overfilling can lead your refrigerator's temperature to drop below safe levels, resulting in food safety problems. I never knew this before I catered. I thought it was fine to stuff as much as possible into my refrigerator as long as I could get the door closed. Another thing I didn't know was that some parts of a refrigerator are less cold than other parts. Commercial refrigerators are designed to prevent this from happening, but if you're using a home refrigerator, you must become acutely aware of these warmer spots. You want to be extremely careful not to put a mayonnaise product such as tuna salad or egg salad in these spots. A long enough time in a just below the safety zone could lead to a food poisoning episode.

Now that we've established how proper kitchen organization and equipment management can contributed to keeping your food safe, it is time to move on to food safety in more depth. Much of what we will cover is common sense, the sort of wisdom that your grandmother passed onto your mother, and she passed onto you. Read on to see which of these old wives' tales regarding food safety are indeed fact and which are fiction.

Take time to reflect on how *you* might want to set up *your* kitchen. As time goes on you will continue to improve your organization and flow. You will make new business decisions about your kitchen space, when to stay where you are, and when you need more space. And always remember:

No kitchen is perfect; all will work.

RECIPE REQUIREMENT: Something that
Gets Better With Age

I don't think I've ever made a soup that wasn't rendered more delicious by spending a few days in the fridge. Making a soup ahead of time allows the flavors to "marry." Get your soups, stews, or étouffées cooked and put away in your fridge several days ahead of your event. Out of sight, out of mind! Right before serving, just taste the soup and re-spice if needed. Then chop up some avocados and you'll be set.

Green Chili Chicken and Lime Soup

INGREDIENTS:
2 tbsp virgin olive oil
I onion chopped
4 cloves garlic
80 oz chicken broth
I0 oz Rotel tomatoes
7 oz canned green chilis
4 boneless chicken breasts
  (cooked and shredded)
2 ½ cups of cooked rice
¼ cup lime juice
I ½ tsp cumin
I or so pinches kosher salt

OPTIONAL TOPPINGS:
chopped cilantro
chopped avocados
tortilla chips
sour cream (add cumin to spice)

In a stock pot, cook the onion in olive oil over medium-low heat for about 5 minutes or until soft and translucent. Add the garlic and cook for I more minute (do not let it brown).

Stir in chicken broth, tomtoes, green chilies, chicken breast, rice, lime juice. Cook for 5 minutes; taste and season accordingly.

Let soup cool to a safe temperature, Refrigerate in sealed containers until the day of the party. Add chopped cilantro before serving.

At your party, put out bowls of chopped avocados, shredded cheese, chopped tortilla chips, chopped cilantro, cumin-spiced sour cream, etc. Guests can dollop their soup with whatever toppings they wish.

CHAPTER ELEVEN
Food Safety

AS A PROFESSIONAL CATERER, YOU ARE ENTRUSTED
WITH PROVIDING HEALTHY AND SAFE FOOD.
IT IS ALWAYS BETTER TO BE SAFE THAN SORRY.

• •

Every year in the United States, approximately forty-eight million people experience foodborne illnesses. Three thousand people die from them! What's worse, statistics from the CDC show that there are more reported outbreaks of food poisoning linked to catering than to restaurants or home cooking.

Imagining some of the worst case scenarios involving foodborne illness may make you wish to put down this book immediately and switch to a retail career, so I'll keep the discussion of the possible devastation brief. Few caterering businesses recover after being involved in an outbreak of foodborne illness. If things escalate to the point where the Department of Health investigates what caused the illness, they will likely find you guilty of *something* and temporarily shut you down, regardless of whether you're operating with a license.

On this note, an important thing to remember is that food safety regulations are constantly changing. In 2011, President Obama signed the Food Safety Modernization Act, giving the FDA the power to make new legislation designed to strengthen the food safety system. At the time that this book went to press, the FDA was in the process of finalizing and implementing many of the new regulations. As a caterer, you are responsible for keeping up-to-date with the rules and regulations that apply to you. The Health Department won't care if you're playing by the rules if the rules in question are outdated.

I am about to provide you with those rules and concepts that I believe are most valuable in keeping food safe. Some are obvious; others are learned over many years, but all these procedures should be kept foremost in your mind while producing any job.

MICRO-ORGANISMS: A CATERER'S WORST ENEMY

All raw food products contain **microorganisms**. The most common types of microorganisms found in food are viruses, bacteria, and yeasts. Not all of these are harmful. Probiotics, for instance, are a type of bacteria found in certain dairy products that can help the human digestive system. And where would be without yeast? We have that microorganism to thank for fluffy breads and strong beers.

But as well all know, microorganisms are capable of doing serious harm. When we talk about this kind of harm, we're really talking about two different things: foodborne illness and food spoilage. Foodborne illness occurs when a person ingests food that's been contaminated by certain bacteria, viruses, parasites, or toxins. Foodborne illness can be unpleasant, deadly, or anything in between. On the other hand, microorganisms like yesats, mold, and some funguses may cause a food product to spoil, but these spoiled foods will not cause illness if ingested.

Viruses and Bacteria

Viruses are the leading cause of foodborne illness. For the most part, **viruses cannot be killed by cooking food nor freezing it.** Viruses can survive for weeks on prep tables, utensils, or in any type of food or drink. It only takes a very small particle of a virus, such as Norovirus or Hepatitis A, to infect a person. If you or your staff is infected with one of these viruses, just touching the vegetables that go into a salad can transmit this illness to any guests who ultimately eat that salad. That is very worrisome, to say the least.

While **bacteria can be killed by cooking food at a high enough temperature** (See page 130 for more), freezing food won't eradicate bacteria. In fact, bacteria will stay in a state of "living suspension" in the freezer and will begin to grow as soon as the food is no longer frozen. What's even more haunting, bacteria can be found literally everywhere: in your kitchen, in your hair, or even on non-potentially hazardous foods.

Whereas viruses can only cause foodborne illness, bacteria, depending on type, can cause either food spoilage or foodborne illness (sometimes the bacteria that cause illness are distinguished by the term "pathogenic bacteria" while those that cause spoilage are called "spoilage bacteria.") As long as bacteria have something to eat and drink, they'll multiply, and when enough bacteria (and enough of their waste products) become present in a food, the food's odor, taste, and texture changes. Bacterial overgrowth is responsible for spoiled milk, slimy fruits, and more.

The Conditions That Encourage Bacterial Growth

The food safety industry has created an acronym to help caterers and chefs remember the conditions that encourage bacterial growth:

food   acidity   temp   time   oxygen   moisture

FOOD: Bacteria need to be fed to grow and survive, just like people. Bacteria can eat anything that is edible to animals or humans, plus lots of things that aren't.

ACIDITY: All foods can be rated according to their pH (acid) levels. The pH scale ranges from 0-14. Below 7 is acidic, above 7 alkaline. If a food's acid level is between 4.6 and 7.5 it is vulnerable to bacteria. On the flip side, very acidic food below 4.6 will actually help prevent some bacteria from growing and even kill some bacteria. Lemons, vinegar and pineapples are some foods in this category.

TEMPERATURE: Bacteria will grow at temperatures between 41 and 135 degrees F. The longer food stays in this "temperature danger zone," the more likely bacteria will grow.

TIME: The maximum time that food can stay in the temperature danger zone is two hours (some say four, but two is safer). This applies to both cooked and ucooked foods. After two hours, the food must be "removed" from the danger zone, either by cooling (in the case of cooked foods) or heating (in the case of uncooked foods).

OXYGEN: Most bacteria require oxygen to survive, but not all do. Those that do, such as staph, are called aerobic bacteria; those that don't, such as e. coli, are called anaerobic bacteria.

MOISTURE: Moisture content is measured using the water activity (a_w) scale, which indicates the amount of free water available in a food for microorganisms to use for growth. The scale ranges from 0.0 to 1.0. Activity levels from .85 to .99 are high and indicate potential danger. Lightly cooked bacon, for example, has a .98 water activity level. If you cook it until very crispy, water activity level drops to around .75, and pathogenic bacteria can no longer grow.

Toxins and Parasites

In addition to viruses and bacteria, there are two main causes of foodborne illness: toxins and parasites. Parasites are worms which settle in an animal or human host and transmit illness. They can be found in certain foods that come from animals. For instance, raw or undercooked pork can contain a parasite that causes an illness called trichinosis. Since parasites can also be hosted by humans, they can be found in human feces (this, ladies and gentleman, is why we wash our hands). Luckily, parasites can be killed by both freezing and cooking.

There are two sources of toxins most commonly implicated in foodborne illness: seafood and mushrooms. In fish or shellfish, contamination is caused by fish eating toxins (or eating smaller fish that previously ate toxins), and thus occurs *before* the fish are caught. Skilled fisherman--the kind who sell their goods to reputable fish markets--now how to avoid catching fish that may be contaminated. Therefore, the best way to avoid buying contaminated seafood is to **only** buy from reputable vendors. Don't skimp on costs when it comes to fish and seafood.

Toxins can also be present in mushrooms. But just as a good fisherman knows the signs of contaminated fish, a good mushroom collector knows which mushrooms are edible and which are toxic. Therefore, buying your mushrooms from a reputable produce vendor is a safe move.

Molds and Yeasts

Fungi such as molds and yeasts are another types of microorganism (mushrooms are fungi too, but a different kind). As any cheese connoisseur will tell you, molds themselves will not make people sick. But molds have the ability to produce toxins that, when ingested, *can* cause illness. For example, the fungus *asperigillus* produces toxins that can be harmful when ingested. *Aspergillus* can contaminate foods like dried beans, cereal grain, peanuts, and oil seeds. As for yeast, it can spoil foods with high sugar content, such as honeys, jams, and juices, or highly acidic foods like tomatoes or pickles.

Looking on the bright side, the good thing about spoilage from molds, yeasts, and spoilage bacteria is that you can tell when it occurs. You can see a patch of mold, curdled milk, or a mushy spot on a peach. On the other hand, you cannot normally tell when a food is carrying a virus, a parasite, toxins, or pathogenic bacteria.

easy to tell the bad apple, right?

Where Micro-Organisms Strike: TCS Foods

Micro-organisms can strike all sorts of food, but some of their favorite targets are a group called **TCS foods**. Note that these were formally known as PHF (Potentially Hazardous Foods), and sometimes the term PHF/TCS is still used.

TCS stands for Temperature Controlled for Safety. The issue is not that there's anything inherently wrong with CS foods themselves, but rather that they are vulnerable to the growth of micro-organisms that cause illness. PHF/TCS foods include:

1) high protein animal products like meat, poultry, dairy, fish and eggs.

2) heat-treated (i.e. cooked) plant foods like vegetables, rice, baked beans, and baked potatoes.

3) other foods such as cut melons, sliced tomatoes, cut leafy greens, tofu and garlic-in-oil mixtures.

All of these are prey to hazardous micro-organisms when sitting at room temperature (between 40 and 140 degrees F)

A MULTI-FRONT ATTACK

Although we've reviewed the microorganisms most commonly re-sponsible food fooborne illess and food spoilage, you probably need a Ph.D. in Biology to really understand the nuances of how these micro-organisms destroy food. What's more important for you, as a caterer or other type of food handler, is knowing how to combat these dangers. Imagine attacking these culprits on three fronts:

the food:	the environment:	the people:
making sure your food is properly cooked, reheat-ed, thawed, and stored.	keeping kitchens and equipment clean and sanitized, whether at home or at a site	prevent staff members from transmitting illness by using proper hygiene practices.

THE FOOD

Cooking Foods

Always use a thermometer to test food you've just cooked. Place it into the core of the food at the deepest point. If the product is oddly shaped, like a turkey, take the temperature in a few different spots. Be cautious when using ae thermometer as it can potentially be a cause of cross-contamination. Sanitize it after every use. And frequently check to make sure that that it is working properly and accurately calibrated.

Minimum Internal Temperatures Required for Safety

Beef Steaks, Roasts, & Chops: 145° F and let stand for 3 minutes

Ground or Mixed Meats (including beef, veal, lamb & poultry): 165°

Pork: 145° and let stand for 3 minutes

Poultry: 165° and make sure to truly check if it's done

Eggs and Egg Dishes: Cook until yolks are yellow and firm

Fin Fish: Cook until flesh is opaque and separates easily with a fork

Shrimp, Lobster, & Crabs: Cook until flesh is pearly and opaque

Crabs, Oysters, Mussels, & Scallops: Cook until flesh is milky white or opaque and firm

---

Holding Food

After your food is cooked to where it has reached a safe internal temperature, it must be properly held in order to remain safe. Cooked food can only remain at room temperature (between 40° and 140°) for two hours before it must be moved to either a hot or cold storage environment. Hot holding environments must have temperatures of 140° or higher. In a cold storage environment, temperatures must be at 40° or below to be safe. If cold food items go above 40° degrees and stay there for over 2 hours, they must be thrown away or immediately restored to safe temperature by being placed in a freezer or ice bath.

For food on a buffet, the same rule applies: cold food must be kept at 40° or colder, and hot foods must be kept at 140° or higher. Using chafing dishes or food warmers can help keep warm food at safe temperatures, but if you're not using these devices, then **food can only remain on a buffet in room temperature for two hours.**

Reheating Food

Now let's move onto guidelines for reheating food. When you are reheating food that was previously cooked and properly held, you have two hours to bring it up to 165°. If you broil the food and get it up to 165° in 5 minutes, that's fine. If you put it over low heat and it takes 1.5 hours to reach 165°, that's fine as well. Once the food is reheated to 165°, you can allow it to cool down to 140° but no lower. Surprisingly, it can stay at 140° (or above) as long as need be before serving it. There is no maximum duration that food can stay at 140° (or above) but there is of course a point where quality diminishes. If hot food drops below 140° (i.e. hits room tempeature) and stays in that zone for over 2 hours, it must be thrown away or reheated back to 165°.

Thawing Food

Have you even thawed ground beef somewhere other than in your refrigerator? On the countertop, perhaps? I imagine that you have, as have I. Once, before I became a professional cook, I forgot to thaw out a turkey, so I thought it would be a great idea to set it on top of the washing machine on Thanksgiving morning. I did this despite the dire warnings not to thaw food outside the refrigerator. I did not heed this warning, and proceeded to keep the turkey on top of the Maytag. Fortunately, no one got sick. I was lucky that time, but it could have been an intestinal disaster and an unforgettable Thanksgiving.

The truth about thawing is that it **is recommended to only thaw in the refrigerator**. There are a few exceptions to this rule. First, you can submerge food completely under non-stop cold running water. Secondly, you can use a microwave (see box on the next page for more).

Cooling Food

Determining the appropriate temperatures for the cooling down process can be confusing. Think of the cooling down process as having two phases:

♦ First, the food must cool down to 70° or lower within two hours.
♦ If you can get the food cooled down to 70° in two hours, you will then have four hours to reduce it from 70° to the preferred 40°.

There are some safe tricks to chilling your food. Place it in shallow pans or separate the food into smaller or thinner portions. You can add ice to the ingredients where it won't affect the quality or stir food with an "ice wand." or "cold paddle." Finally, you could cover food loosely, but not so loose that contaminants would fall in.

Should a hot large pot of chili be placed in the refrigerator after it

A fresh baked item such as a pie
needs to cool down before it's safe
to refrigerate.

has been made? The answer is absolutely not! Why? There is no telling what bacteria could brew in the time it would take to drop to the safe temperature of 41 degrees or below. Also, even if the actual item you placed in the refrigerator did cool down sufficiently in the allowed six hour process, the heat radiating from that item might have increased the nearby air temperature to over 41 degrees, putting adjacent foods in the danger zone. So when can you refrigerator your items? Once the food has reached 70 degrees in the allotted two hours, you can put that item in the refrigerator. It can finish cooling down in the remaining four hours. You may want to leave it partially uncovered to cool down, but don't forget to cover it all the way after the four hours have lapsed.

Storing Dry Goods

Dry goods also have safety and storage restrictions. Guess how far off the ground your products are required to be. Six inches! The exception to the six inches regulation is plastic crates that can be stored on an immaculate floor. Do not store food and equipment where they are likely to get moist and potentially wet. Also, it is important that you rotate your products by using the FIFO method. What is that you ask? It stands for first in, first out. Use your oldest items first, your newest last. This is true for cans, dry ingredients, and refrigerator items. Set up a system that deals with usage by age of product. Common sense dictates that all food should be covered tightly when in storage and kept at a temperature between 50 and 70 degrees.

Storing Refrigerated Foods

Food must always be stored below 41 degrees in a refrigerator. Preferably the air in the fridge is 38 to 39 degrees. Periodically check the temperature of both the air and your products. The shelves in your refrigerator should not be solid, but preferable open grated in order to allow air to circulate freely. As for safe refrigeration times, it is recommended that ready-to-eat food can be left in your fridge for up to seven days as long as the temp is checked and stays below 41 degrees. What about your freezer? Maintain the temperature at zero degrees and periodically check to make sure that your items are frozen.

There actually is a safe order to storing food in your fridge. Uncooked poultry should be at the bottom level. On the next level up, place ground meats and fish. Next place the whole cuts of beef and pork, then whole fish and finally, on the top shelf, ready-to-eat foods.

Safely Using a Microwave

- The risk of thawing in the microwave is that the outer edges of the food will become cooked while the insides remain frozen,
- When defrosting items that are frozen together (such as a package of chicken breasts), separate them as they thaw.
- Food that's thawed in the microwave must be cooked immediately afterward. Once cooked, it can be refrozen safely.
- Food must be kept covered, rotated, and stirred several times throughout the microwave process.
- When using a microwave for reheating, the food being reheated has to reach 165°F and then stand for 2 minutes.

THE ENVIRONMENT

A clean and sanitary kitchen is essential to food safety. After all, a batch of cooked chicken breasts that are been perfectly safe to eat can easily become contaminated if placed in an unclean serving dish.

The Three Bay Sink Method of Cleaning and Sanitizing

Below you will find the five steps of effective cleaning and sanitizing.

1. Scrape all food and debris into the trash
2. Clean items with a brush, cloth, or nylon scrub pad in soapy water of at least 110 degrees in sink.
3. Rinse in fresh water in sink.
4. Sanitize with industrial chemical cleaner in sink.
5. Air dry on drying rack or hanging rack. Do not dry with a towel but if need be, use a fresh paper towel instead.

Cleaning Versus Sanitizing Agents

What is the difference between cleaning agents and sanitizing agents? Cleaning agents help remove food debris or soil from plates, utensils, cutting boards or just about any other surface in the kitchen. They are detergents that when combined with hot water remove food or grime from surfaces. De-greasers are cleaning agents that re-move heavy grease buildup. There are acidic cleaning agents for cleaning mineral deposit buildup and abrasive cleaning agents for surfaces with heavy, baked/cooked on foods such as sauces on the bottom of sauté pans. On the other hand, sanitizing is the process of killing most patho-genic microorganisms. Even though a surface is cleaned, there may still be microscopic organisms existing on it that are invisible to the human eye. You can sanitize a surface or object by using either heat or chemi-cal methods, but only after you have properly cleaned and rinsed it.

> **Battle of the Sanitizing Methods...**
>
> You can use heat to sanitize items in a Three Bay Sink by immersing them in water of 171 degrees for at least 30 seconds, yet it can be difficult to main-tain water at this temperature and hard to touch dishes in water this hot. It is easier to use dishwashers with water temperatures of 180 degrees for sanitizing instead.

Most caterers who do not have large commercial kitchens with dishwashers tend to use chemicals for sanitizing. The names of the sanitizing chemicals typically recommended are Quats, Iodine or Chlorine. These industrial chemicals are used with important directions specifying the concentration of the chemicals to be used. Too much of the sanitizing solution can be toxic to humans; not enough can allow the micro-organisms to continue to exist. Concentrations are always listed in PPMs (parts per million). You are instructed on the bottle how much chemical to use with a specific quantity of water at a specific temperature. You are then required to check for the accurate solutions with specific test strips. When you have achieved the right solution, the color will be correct on the strip. If not, you will either need to add more water or more chemicals until you have it correct.

Finally, all of your CIP (cleaning in place) equipment must be cleaned and sanitized on a regular basis. It does not have to be a daily chore. It is important to establish a regular schedule of cleaning and sanitizing your refrigerator, handles, food processor, etc. to ensure the safest cooking and production environment.

Food Safety at the Event

The necessity of keeping the environment safe for food doesn't stop when you pack up your food and leave your kitchen. If anything, it becomes more important to practice sanitation measures outside of your own kitchen! Envision catering an outdoor party—can you imagine how much more complicated safety becomes when you add in factors like bugs, pollen, and unpredictable temperatures?

Even before you travel to the event site, you need to make the vehicle you'll be using to transport your food into a safe and sanitary environment. As a small caterer, you'll likely use your vehicle for multiple purposes. If you go camping one weekend and cater a job the next, that car interior could easy be contaminated!

Guests at a party may want to reuse their same plate to return to the buffet table. Our staff will often encourage them to get a new plate for their "second time around." Why? If they were to have a virus, their utensil or plate might accidentally touch the utensils or foods on the buffet spreading the virus.

This isn't the time or place for me to go into more detail about food safety at the event, but I'll leave you with this thought. As a caterer, you are ultimately responsible for the safety of the guests. It doesn't matter if your food picks up a micro-organism from the tap water at a function hall or falls out of the safety zone due to a client's faulty freezer. If someone gets sick, you are responsible.

THE PEOPLE

Handwashing

If it seems like you are doing more handwashing than cooking, that's a good sign! But are you actually washing your hands correctly? Read the FDA guidelines in the box below and see how your technique compares. According to the FDA, it should take you twenty seconds to wash your hands. And the twenty seconds doesn't include turning on the faucet or drying your skin: **you must actually keep your hands in soap and water for twenty seconds!** Who knew? When I first started catering, I thought I followed the hand-washing rule, but my version of proper hand-washing meant speeding through the process and grabbing a cloth or towel to dry my hands.

The FDA's Official Guidelines for Handwashing

The How: Turn on a comfortable hot water temperature, apply a generous portion of liquid soap, generate a heavy lather, and rinse well for 20 seconds. Wash between your fingers, under fingernails, and don't forget the back of your hands. Hold your hands so water flows downward from your wrists to your fingertips. Dry your hands with only paper towel, and use this paper towel to turn off the faucet.

The When: Wash your hands when doing any of the following:
1. When you first arrive at work
2. Before and after touching raw foods, including eggs
3. After using the restroom
4. After touching any part of your body
5. After doing activities such as sweeping the floor, taking out trash, eating or drinking, and even after washing dirty dishes.

Sanitation Gloves

Most health departments require using gloves during food preparation and while serving food. It is recommended that you wash your hands both before and after you put on your gloves and between glove changes. The general rule is that bare hand contact with "ready to eat" foods should be avoided by using gloves, deli tissues, serving utensils.

Although there are many good reasons for using them in your cooking and serving, I have noticed that gloves can sometimes give your staff a false sense of cleanliness and safety. They forget to switch their gloves between tasks, thinking that as long as they've got gloves on, they are safe to do anything. They are not! Remind staff to be vigilant when it comes to using gloves. Ultimately, as the boss, you are responsible if your food causes any health problems.

The public is very sensitive to the media coverage of potential pandemics and viruses, and therefore, they are very aware of the importance of food handlers' glove usage. Your clients may have strong opinions about the usage of gloves with their guests. It's not a bad idea to find out their preferences and make a decision accordingly.

Be Careful When....

Pushing Your Buttons

Handles and knobs—such as those on faucets, refrigerators, stove doors, food processors, etc.—are breeding grounds for contamination. Keep them clean! Visualize yourself preparing fish filet with coconut panko crumbs. Suddenly you remember that you need to warm the butter for a buttercream icing. It is a lot closer to reach for the refrigerator handle than to take the extra steps to the sink and follow hand washing procedures. As a result, the bacteria from the fish stays on the refrigerator, the kitchen heats up, you touch that same handle to take out a lime for the salad dressing, cut it, and squeeze it with the same hand. Cross contamination is now everywhere! Try tracing your steps one day while preparing dinner for your family. How many times are you guilty of touching surfaces with raw products that will generate all kinds of dangerous microorganisms? Scary? Indeed!

Safe Work Attire

Do you need to purchase a chef jacket to be worn while preparing or serving your jobs? You can if you wish, but it is not a necessity. Wearing clean outer clothing, such as an apron, is important. Don't wear baggy or loose clothing. Clothes can catch on fire more easily than you'd think: when you are busy on a job, it is easy to accidentally put your loose sleeve over the gas stove! Avoid this by wearing fitted outfits. No jewelry should be worn, as jewelry not only harbors bacteria but may drop into your food or equipment as well. Always keep your hair pulled back or up. You don't need a hairnet, but your hair can't be loose. It is always best to do all you can to make sure that nothing falls into your food except great spices and seasonings!

Drinking on the Job

Water, that is! Interestingly enough, some health departments don't even allow this; under their rules, you would have to go into another room to hydrate yourself. Others say you can drink a beverage if it is stored in a cup with a lid and a straw in order to prevent the contamination of food and equipment.

Certainly, as an extension of the no-drinking rule, you should not eat lunch or snack in your kitchen! But this begs the question: **Don't I need to taste the food I am preparing?** How many thousands of times have we taken a little taste of the soup over the pot? Instead, make a habit of putting a small amount of food in a container and going off to the side to taste it. Use inexpensive Dixie cups and plastic spoons. Although this step may seem time-consuming, think about how your clients would react if they knew that your fingers had been in the food. Be respectful and be safe.

Thinking of eating right off the spoon? What would your client say if she knew?

TEST TIME!

You're not being tested on the information in this chapter... yet. But once your company is officially open for business, you and/or your staff members will likely be required to obtain a food safety certification, and that does entail passing an examination. Depending on what state you live in, there will be different accredited programs from which you can choose. One of the most popular programs, ServSafe, is recognized nationwide. The advantage of taking a program that's accredited in all states is that, should you ever move, you won't have to retake the course. The ServSafe course may be taken independently (either online or in print) or in a classroom. The testing fees are relatively low-cost (typically ranging from $40 to $100). These tests are generally manageable and easily completed with a very high pass rate.

When you look into the requirements for food-safety certification, you will likely come across the wording "person-in-charge." Many state health codes stipulate that a food establishment need to have a designated person-in-charge on site at all times, and that that person **must** be safety certified. In other words, these codes do not require *all* food handlers to have safety certification, so long as there is a certified person-in-charge. Don't take this to mean that if your chef has a food safety-certification, it is unnecessary for you or any other staff members to have one. If there's ever a time when the chef is offsite and there's no safety-certified employee who can act as the person-in-charge at establishment, you could be in trouble.

This chapter was packed with information, none of which has been very "sexy," to say the least! To supplement what you've learned here, schedule a visit with a caterer or a restaurant and observe their safety practices. If you couple real-world kitchen experience with the information provided here and with knowledge gained in a food safety course, you will naturally start to implement the necessary safety procedures. Soon food safety will be second nature.

CHAPTER TWELVE
Cooking in Quantities

NOT THE WHO BUT THE HOW...
HOW TO AND HOW MUCH.

· ·

When people hear that I am a caterer, they exclaim, "How in the world do you know how to cook for so many people? I could never do that"! My response is, "Yes, you can"! Once I took the fear out of the equation, cooking for 200 began to feel like cooking for 20. If you've managed a dinner party for 20, you can easily learn to cook for 200. Still not convinced? This chapter will shed light on a number of ways to make a seemingly daunting experience manageable.

Before we go into the details how to cook in large quantities, let me stress the importance of organization. This, more than anything else, will help your cooking go smoothly. Your prep list will set forth the quantities that you will need to produce of each recipe. This will then help you determine how you will allocate and schedule your pots and pans for production. For example, say you need to cook 100 servings of rice with a pot that only cooks 10 servings at a time. You will need to cook 10 batches of rice. If each pot takes 20 minutes to prepare, it will take 200 minutes, or $3^{1}/_{3}$ hours, of cooking to get it all done. It will be critical that you consider what other tasks you can complete during the time that your rice pot is occupied. Also, you need to go over what other menu items you *do* need that pot for, and schedule a different time to get them done. In essence, you are actually scheduling your pots and pans as well as your items to be prepared.

HOW TO COOK IN LARGE QUANTITIES

Choosing Your Equipment

In the example just discussed, the limited size of your pot required you to cook your rice in ten separate batches. But would you really choose a larger pot, if you could? Industry chefs and cooks who use larger industrial pots and pans frequently comment on the challenge of maintaining the essence of the original recipe. And after all these years, I still find that I have a tendency to either overcook or even burn food when using large industrial pots.

My recommendation is that you choose the largest pots and pans with which you are comfortable. Obviously, the larger pot you are comfortable cooking with, the less time you will have to repeat cooking the same recipe. If you have the opportunity to borrow larger pots and pans and try them out, you may want to do this, just not when you're preparing for an actual catering function. This will give you a sense of whether you want to cook with larger sized pots and pans or if you prefer to stay with the size you have in your collection. Keep experimenting and keep your ears and eyes open for different size and kinds of pans. No matter how large your business grows, you may discover that the pots you already own are the very ones that work best for you.

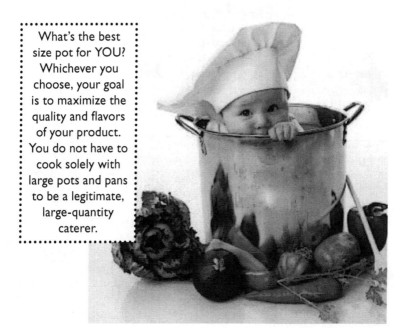

What's the best size pot for YOU? Whichever you choose, your goal is to maximize the quality and flavors of your product. You do not have to cook solely with large pots and pans to be a legitimate, large-quantity caterer.

Batch Cooking

If you decide to use regular-sized pots, you will then need to produce your quantities in sequential cooking. This is referred to in the industry as "batch cooking." Batch cooking requires a little planning, but it also comes with advantages/ The beauty of batch cooking for large quantities is that it produces enough to feed hundreds while retaining the essence and flavor of cooking for twenty.

As for the disadvantages of batch cooking, the primary one is that it takes more time. But if you multi-task effectively, then cooking with pots that can only produce small quantities need not slow you down. For example, in the time that your ten batches of rice are simmering, you can make a paste for your chicken in the food processor and use your oven to roast your vegetables. With time, you will become savvy at both planning your production and multi tasking.

Making Adjustments

As you cook larger quantities, you will notice that your cooking time may take longer. **As the volume of food and the surface area of your pots increase, your cooking time will probably increase.** This is something you will learn to accomodate for over time.

There's nothing like hands-on experimentation to help you get used to adjusting your cooking technique based on the quantities you're preparing. You might try the following: Make a meat sauce for 10 people. Notice how long this process takes you and what temperature you need. Now, get out a larger pan and set out to make enough sauce for 30 people. What do you need to do in order to cook the larger batch? Do you have to raise the heat to begin sauteeing the meat? How much more cooking time is needed?

The *art* of cooking in quantities is knowing how to SEQUENCE & TIME your recipes.

Perhaps the most surprising and counterintuitive part of cooking in quantities is that **when you multiply your original recipe to obtain the quantity that you need to achieve, you should not necessarily multiply all ingredients in the recipe times the quantity variable you are working with**. For example, if you are making a stew for 60 with a recipe for ten servings, you will multiply the beef quantity by 6, but you won't need six times the amount of salt, pepper, herbs and oils. Other ingredients will also vary. For example, if the stew recipe for ten servings calls for one can of tomatoes, then when making enough for sixty, start with four cans of tomatoes, not six. Taste the stew and adjust accordingly. You *may* end up using all six cans, but you may not. Go slow. Taste. Observe. Add where needed.

Quantity Cooking: An Art, Not a Science:

While learning how to cook in large quantities, I became intrigued with the finesse involved. I wondered why there wasn't a definitive algorithim for convering measurements when increasing ingredients. My curiosity lead me to conversations with chefs and cooks. To my relief, all of them could relate to my observations. Some had just accepted this phenomenon as reality, while others attributed it to "kitchen chemistry." They explained how the chemical makeup is different for every raw product (e.g. mint and rosemary will have different chemical makeups). Even the manufactured products amongst manufacturers will have different chemical makeups (e.g. King Arthur's flour isn't identical to Pillsbury). These different chemical structures when heated, whisked, blended, etc. will come together at different times and in different ways.

Does this sound familiar? You're making your favorite tomato sauce, and you will notice your ingredients coming together seemingly with perfect liquidity and taste. However, the quantity looks a little short! You add in another round of each ingredient, and... oops! Those two cans of tomato paste and basil seems to have shifted the perfection you had achieved. What was the cause of this? There is a distinct saturation point in the emulsification (or coming together) of all ingredients. Any ingredients that you add after this point, will act like "extras," and the overall taste and texture of your product will be affected.

Safety When Cooking Large Quantities

When preparing large quantities of food, a professional cook must be more mindful about how to handle the food after cooking. The most important rule is to **cool your cooked food as quickly as possible so that it will be out of the temperature danger zone as soon as possible**. Some chefs use ice baths to bring down temperatures quickly, and large kitchens may come equipped with commercial refrigerators with special cooling systems that allow you to put away the food "as is" (see Page 135 if you need a reminder of why this is unsafe to do in a typical fridge). If you don't have access to these technologies, however, the best approach is to divide up your food into smaller quantities and cool it down in shallow pans. Obviously a large quantity of food kept together in one huge pot will take it significantly longer to cool down than several small quantities spread across multiple pots or several sheet pans.

Another advantage of batch cooking becomes apparent here. Not only does batch cooking allow you to control the quality of your food, but small batches translate to quicker cool down times, making your safety concerns less complicated. Say you need to make four gallons of soup. If you used a five gallon industrial pot, you could make the whole batch in one go, but unless you divided the soup into smaller quantities, it would not cool quickly enough to meet safety standards. You would need to pour the soup into smaller containers—a messy endeavor—in order to make sure it cools quickly enough.

Now imagine cooking with a single gallon pot. When you finish that first pot of soup, you pour the soup into a large ceramic bowl to cool, and you get Pot 2 going on the stove. By the time Pot 2 is ready to be taken off the heat, the soup in the ceramic bowl will have cooled to under 41 degrees, making it safe for refrigeration. It'll be easy to transfer that gallon of soup from the ceramic bowl into plastic containers and store those containers in the fridge. You then move the contents of Pot 2 into the ceramic bowl and start on Pot 3. By the time you finish cooking Pot 3, you can move Pot 2 into the fridge. You get the idea.

HOW MUCH FOOD IS ENOUGH– AND IS ENOUGH REALLY ENOUGH?

Next to "How *can* you cook enough food for 200 people?", the question I hear most frequently, "How in the world do you know *how much* to cook for so many guests?" The answer? I don't know, not exactly. **Knowing how much food I need is a sensibility that has taken me a lot of time and experience to develop, and remains imperfect .**

I want there to be zero possibility of running out of food. This, more than anything else, guides my calculations. If I have determined that five heads of romaine lettuce are enough to make a Caesar salad for twenty-five ladies, I'll purchase six heads. **As experienced as I've become at estimating food quantities, I always add extra so that I don't run out of food.**

There are so many variables affecting what quantities a party will require that you can't ever really know how much you need. All you can do is to be cognizant of these variables and consider them as you are shopping. In the coming pages, I'll go over four of those variables:

+ Demographics
+ Time of Day
+ The Sequence of the Menu
+ Yield Versus Poundage

Demographics

First of all, consider the demographics of your party: what are the ages, cultures, even the occupations of the guests? If you are catering fhe 80th birthday celebration of a local TV commentator, you will calculate on the conservative side of your estimated quantities, as elderly people tend to eat less. But perhaps you've noted that elderly persons tend to really enjoy desserts. You will then increase your production of those. If you are catering for a party of 13-year-olds, increase your purchase of chips and salsa. If the hostess wants you to serve broccoli with pasta at the same party, buy enough broccoli, but just enough. If meat is on the menu at a bachelor party for thirty-something men, buy a lot of it. I guarantee there won't be much left.

Different ethnic cultures eat differently. If you're catering a Buddhist reception, you would be more likely to increase your proportion of vegetables and grains, even if animal protein were included in the menu. Be aware of such details when constructing your shopping list. If you do not know a particular culture's likes and dislikes, you may want to ask your client (just make sure the moment is right). You can also do a little research on the culture.

Time of Day

The time of day at which your party takes place will affect your quantities. For the most part, people will eat somewhat less at lunch time than in the evening. However, I've seen quite a quantity be eaten during an afternoon event. This is especially true if the lunch follows a religious service or other type of ceremony; when people have been sitting in near silence for hours, trying to ignore their rumbling stomachs, they'll eat quite eagerly as soon as they get the chance.

The Sequence of the Menu

To know the required quantity of a particular item, you must look at where each item on your menu is positioned. If your hostess has requested a long appetizer period, you will increase your quantity of appetizers while slightly reducing the quantity of food in the main course. But it's not that simple: there are always multiple factors that should be taken into consideration. Say there is a long pause, perhaps an hour presentation, between the appetizer course and the main. In this case, be wary of decreasing the quantity of main course foods: after an hour of sitting, your guests have worked up an appetite. If you cut back, you may run short.

Let's go over another example. At Miss Jeanies, we frequently have an extended appetizer period comprised of multiple interactive stations. The opportunity to have a custom appetizer such as a spring roll or a fritter cooked for you on the stop is a difficult one to pass up. So a guest tries out the springroll bar. Next, she heads to the fritter station and asks for a corn fritter. She joins a friend at a cocktail table, and that friend says to her, "Did you get zucchini in your fritter? You MUST." She heads back to the fritter station. In addition to the interactive stations, appetizers are being passed around on trays. At such parties, by the time we offer the "main course", guests have begun to notice their waistbands getting tighter. In this scenario, I can comfortably cut back on the amount of main course food I serve. Contrast this to a party that has just three passed appetizers immediately followed by a main course buffet. Even if both parties had an identical number of guests, I would prepare a **much** larger quantity of the main course foods at the latter.

These scenarios have been focusing on buffets or stations. When you are offering a plated main course dinner, you are able to calculate your needed quantities more precisely. If you are offering a bundle of 5 asparagus spears on each plate, and you're making 100 plates, you purchase 500 asparagus (plus a few extra, just in case). If you are offering a tenderloin, and you decide to plate 3 slices per person, you just need to calculate how many servable slices you can cut from a pound of tenderloin in order to determine the number of tenderloins to purchase. We'll get to that next.

Yield Versus Poundage

The fourth variable in figuring out quantities is product yield. Yield is different than poundage. If you decide to offer $1/3$ of a pound of beef per person and the tenderloins you see at the market weigh two pounds each, you must consider how much of the tenderloin will be of servable quality. A two pound tenderloin won't yield six $1/3$ pound servings, because some of the meat will always be unusable. You'd wind up short some servings. If you purchased your asparagus by their poundage, you

The important question is: What will those potatoes weigh AFTER they're peeled?

would need to factor in that you will cut off the bottom stems from each asparagus. On the other hand, the yield of something like pasta could be estimated exactly by the pound, as there is no waste. You don't have to think about trimming the ends off pasta, after all.

If you eventually choose to call in your orders to purveyors, you will need to think more precisely in terms of yields rather than poundage, as you'll need to give the purveyor concrete numbers. I've always found working with purveyors a little difficult, as you lose the opportunity to eyeball your quantities. I feel the need to actually see the quantity of food I am purchasing to assure myself I've both purchased enough and purchased the best quality available. Other caterers, however, love how purveyors save them time and energy.

10 Guidelines for Estimating Quantities

There is no foolproof formula for determining the quantity of food you will serve at the parties you cater but here are some possible rules of thumb for figuring out food quantities for your parties:

1. At a buffet, people will want to try a little of everything. Therefore, the more options you have, the less you need of each.

2. People will protest they don't want dessert, but they will eventually want to eat it.

3. Adding bulk items such as bread, olives, nuts, or pretzels increases the surety that you'll have an adequate supply of food.

4. People tend to eat more starches and meats at parties, but fewer salads and vegetables. Fried foods go first. A party mentality makes people less calorie-conscious then normal.

5. If you have more singles than couples, add extra food. Singles don't tend to cook for themselves, so they eat more at a party.

6. People eat more food when it is set out on a platter than when passed around.

7. If people linger at the party, they'll keep eating, even if full.

8. At events with a large number of guests, people tend to eat less.

9. Expensive foods will be all consumed, no matter how much you put out. Usual portion estimates don't count here.

10. Always round your quantity estimates up, never down!!!

Where to Find Advice on Quantities

As you have learned from reading this chapter, there is no foolproof formula for determining the quantity of food you will serve at the parties you cater. Nonetheless, a look through the web reveals an abundance of suggestions for food and beverage quantities. I find the most helpful recommendations to be those that break quantities down to a party of one. For example, here's what a single guest might consume at a party featuring appetizers followed by a main course:

* 6-8 appetizer pieces (at a party with appetizers only, people eat closer to 12-15 appetizer pieces)
* 1 cup of soup
* 1 cup of salad
* 6 oz of meat (or 5 oz if there's more than one main entree)
* 4 oz of starch (potato/rice/pasta)
* 4 oz of vegetables
* 1 piece of dessert

If you really delve into party-planning or catering resources, you can find much more specific guidelines. Ever wondered how many chicken wings you'd need to serve 50 people at a late-afternoon BBQ pool party? That information is probably online somewhere, and there will be times when such expertise is exactly what you need. If you're a brunch expert catering a BBQ for the first time, then by all means, use that guidance! Ultimately, though, your aim should be to develop your own sensibility. **When it comes to deciding the amount of food to serve (and whether to risk running out), be your own most trusted guide.**

CHAPTER THIRTEEN

Honing Your Entrepreneurial and Business Skills

YOU ARE THE CEO OF YOUR COMPANY. YOU'RE ALSO THE CFO, MARKETING DIRECTOR, OFFICE MANAGER, & HEAD OF LEGAL. WHEW!

No matter how large or small your company, you will be its CEO.
Its degree of success or failure is your responsibility.

It took many years of business before I came to think of myself as the CEO of Miss Jeanies. **Even after I finally recognized my business as a business, myself as the owner, I still would not have called myself the CEO.** But looking back, I see that I bore the same responsibilities as an executive of a multi-million dollar corporation, such as setting and monitoring business goals, cultivating a strong staff, etc. The difference between us? In a huge company, the CEO's job description stops at these sorts of executive functions. In a small company, the CEO wears many other hats. In the following pages, we'll talk about five of the roles that you'll fill as CEO and owner:

Leader of Yourself and Your Staff

Chief Financial Officer

Marketing and Advertising Director

Office and Administrative Manager

Head of Legal Department

LEADERSHIP

As the owner of a small business, you will use your leadership skills to nurture your company, earn your clients' respect and loyalty, and eventually, to build a dedicated and reliable team of employees.

Leader of Yourself

As the CEO of your company, you must call forth your leadership skills. You will likely start off leading a team of just one: yourself!

One of your primary responsibilities as a leader will be building a client base. From day one, you must be highly dedicated to creating and nurturing your brand and reputation in order to find clients and keep them coming back for more. You can have the greatest brand and business cards in the city, and market at every opportunity you see, but if you don't maintain your reputation as leader of your company, as well as your company's overall reputation, success will elude you.

Being impeccably honest with clients and transparent in your business transactions are critical first steps in fostering your brand. Every client, or potential client, needs to feel your personal sincerity and investment in your business and in them. All it takes is one client suspecting any sort of deception, whether monetary or operational, and your blossoming company can come to a screeching halt. Clients are savvy and sharp. Any hint of insincerity will be detected. Any weakness

WHAT DOES IT TAKE TO BE A *Leader*?

• You must develop a vision for your company, and make sure that vision remains alive, exciting, and profitable!

• You must begin to set goals for yourself and work extraordinarily hard to achieve them.

• You must make decisions.

• You must solicit aid and support from others when necessary

• You must develop and master competency in your catering tasks and the culinary world

• You must serve as the face of your company, inspiring customers to use your services.

• You must have the belief that you are (for the most part) in control of your destiny. No small feat, for sure, but possible, realistic and empowering!

on your part, however minor, will be registered. You must be aware of these pitfalls and monitor them. Even if a client is delighted by nine out of the ten aspects of your product, that single gripe can disproportionately affect their overall satisfaction. And when that client is asked if he'd recommend your services, he may be too hung up on the one issue to give you the kind of unqualified referral you need.

Historically, my own weak spot was not returning phone calls as quickly as I should. I am certain that over the years, many rave reviews of our parties were delivered with the disclaimer, "She's great, but try getting her to call you back!" No matter how wonderful client reviews were, this message may have lost me clients. At the time, I was managing kids, family, and my career as a therapist. Although I could forgive myself for this lack of punctuality, I was still aware of its consequences.

TAKE A LOOK IN THE Mirror....

A strong entrepreneurial leader will continuously evaluate not only their product, but their personal successes and failures. Introspection and reflection are necessary in order to improve all processes involving your company. Once your business is up and running, ask yourself some of the following questions, and answer honestly:

What mistakes do you continue to make?
Are you too nice to your employees?
Are you too critical when under pressure?
Do you pay your vendors on time?
Do you have difficulty hearing and responding to criticism?
Do you need to be right too often?
When your vision is off, do you tweak it as needed?
Do you allow yourself time to reflect, think, contemplate?
Are you working your very hardest? Truly?
Are you eating well and exercising?
Do you make time for family and friends?
Do you make sure you are rested and calm prior to an event?

Leader of Your Staff

Do not underestimate the value of your staff. They are an integral part of your company's success. As their leader, you will instruct and guide your staff with the vision of how your product will be produced. Lead by example. Set expectations for hard work and dedication.

As testament to the strength of my staff, I typically receive a phone call or an e-mail from the client within a day after the job. Many times the first comment out of the client's mouth—before she gets to praising the design and food—is a compliment on the amazing group of staff I have. "They were attentive to detail! They were gracious to me and my guests!" Miss Jeanies could not have built the reputation it has without its staff. Whether someone works with me for years or does an extraordinary job a single time, their contribution to the company is invaluable.

It was a challenge for me to hire my first staff member. My family members would have loved to join in on the fun; this was impossible, however, as they lived thousands of miles away in Louisiana. My friends—the few who didn't fear cooking—were working, raising kids, or both. What was I to do? I inquired with the staff at my sons' after-school program. I was lucky to discover that the head of the program not only loved to cook but was a dynamite person as well. The concept of helping me with catering sounded magical to her. Young, single, and energetic, she was able to work long hours with me, producing the food for the weekend jobs. Once the weekend came, we would busy ourselves loading my minivan with our culinary delights. Off we went, excited, energized, and exuberant. We set up, served the food, cleaned up and headed back home. Just the two of us. We had a blast. We were exhausted. We were successful!

You too will eventually find a right-hand man or woman to be your first employee. This second-in-command must be a competent, responsible, reliable person whom you trust implicitly. They may be your mother, your sister, or your best friend. Do not be surprised if you go through several people before one "sticks." Someone can seem like the whole package—cooks well, works hard, excellent people skills—but they may just not be the right match for you.

Five Tips For Managing Staff

1	2	3	4	5
Explain directly and emphatically the specific and concrete expectations you have for the job at hand.	Some staff respond well to continuous praise; others want realistic feedback on mistakes as well.	Some staff may not be a match for your company. Accept that. Let them go and pursue others who fit better.	Make sure that your staff is well mannered, courteous, friendly, well dressed and engaging.	Don't forget to keep an up to date staff directory: names, addresses, e-mails, and cell phones.

How to Hire Staff: How do you hire competent staff? I am famous for chatting with people all the time in my daily comings and goings. My staff finds it quite humorous that while running an errand I come back having found a few new recruits in the checkout line. This is one fun way to hire. It's informal, casual, and often effective.

Despite my propensity to scout out up staff members "off the street", I think the best source of acquiring staff is through word of mouth. If a current staff member has a friend who loves food and is looking for work—voilà!...a new member of Miss Jeanies is born! Word of mouth works beautifully and often produces generations of staff whose efficiency, dedication, and loyalty form the core of the company.

Occasionally the word of mouth system will run its course, and you'll need to consider advertising. The disadvantage of using a catch-all tool like online advertising is that you'll get flooded with replies from people with zero interest in catering who systematically respond to every ad they see. Instead, consider these more-specific searches:

+ Post ads directed toward floor staff at colleges and universities. Intermittent work that doesn't require committing to a weekly schedule can be a perfect fit for the busy and unpredictable lives of college or graduate students.
+ Find foodies by running "Help Wanted" ads at local culinary schools, high school culinary programs, or Adult Ed cooking programs.
+ Check out a temp agency when you need a "pre-approved", well-recommended employee in a pinch. The catch? The cost. If you want that employee to earn as much as your other staff members, you'll need to pay them a higher rate, as the temp agency will take a cut of their earnings.

How Much to Pay Your Staff? In order to know how much to pay your staff, start by exploring going rates for different event staff positions. You can look at ads online to see what rates are being offered in your area. You can also ask the people whom you hire, or whom you might hire, what they made elsewhere.

My belief is to be as generous as you possibly can with your staff. Staff who you can count on and who care about your company, nearly as much as you do, are priceless.

As I mentioned in Chapter 7 (see Page 78), it is necessary to budget your staff at slightly higher hourly rate than the staff members may actually receive. This extra money is a form of financial protection. Remember that you may prepare client proposal a year ahead of an event. Imagine that you state on the proposal that the floor staff at a six-hour event will be billed at $16/hour each. A few days before the event, however, one of your $16/hour employees has a family emergency, and you're forced to find a replacement. A trusted senior member of your staff is available to work the floor. However, since that employee earns $20/hour, you're going to need extra money to cover the difference. If you're in the habit of slightly marking up your staff costs, you will have built a fund from which you can withdraw money in cases like this.

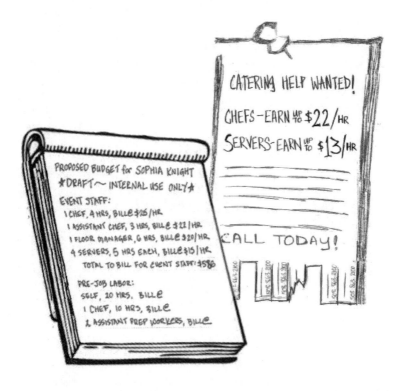

Staff Policies and Agreements: As your business grows, the makeup of your staff will inevitably shift. In all likelihood, you will begin to hire people other than family members or close friends. Additionally, you may eventually hire one or more full-time employees. This is when it becomes necessary to craft more formal staff policies. There are no industry standards for these expectations. You define the expectations for your staff, and your brand is then defined by how your staff comport themselves. Topics you may want to address include dress codes and uniforms, tardiness, cancellations, and drug and alcohol abuse. You may also think about what to do if a staff member violates your policies.

CFO

As Chief Financial Officer, you will manage the finances of your catering business. You must learn to be vigilant when dealing with money.

Your Business Plan

If you are planning to borrow money from a bank or other lending institution, you will need a formal business plan. But even if you do not plan to borrow money, you may still want to write a modified business plan. This will serve as a map, showing you where to begin and where you hope to go.

> What to Include In ...
>
> ## *Your Business Plan*
>
> your widest vision & your plans for reaching this vision
>
> how you will fund your business
>
> your initial marketing plans
>
> your initial expenditures
>
> how much money you hope to earn as profit in the first 3 months, 6 months, or year.
>
> who you will use for advice
>
> how will you assess & handle your competition

Money Management

Although you need some sort of system to effectively manage your company, it need not be elaborate. Open a business banking account as soon as you can, and keep it totally separate from your personal account(s). Use it to deposit monies from your clients and to pay any non-cash transactions.

Next, set up a bookkeeping system. You may do this on your own—either manually or using computer software—or you can hire someone to keep the books. If you're truly abysmal at finances, hiring a good bookkeeper may turn out to be an expense that ultimately *saves* you money.

The basic point of a bookkeeping system is to record everything that comes in and everything that goes out. When recording your business expenditures, organize them into categories, such as:

♦   equipment
♦   gasoline and other transportation costs
♦   rent, utilities, repairs or even renovations for your cooking space
♦   accountant and lawyer fees
♦   office supplies and technology
♦   miscellaneous expenses

At first this level of detail may seem like overkill, but before you know it you will need to compare your spending and budgets and report on your earnings for tax purposes. Thorough and consistent record keeping will aid you in this process.

Funding Your Venture

It may not cost you anything to cater your first job. If your client gives you a deposit, you can use that money to purchase the food and pay the staff for her event. But there may come a time when a small leap will be needed to get your business to the next level. At that time, you may need to look for extra cash.

If at all possible, do not load up your credit card with expenses. Interest is astronomical and you will end up owing incredible amounts of money to the credit card company. If you have a savings account, borrow funds from it instead. It may be scary, but at least you will not be paying interest charges and risking possible bad credit. Keep yourself out of debt as much as possible.

A traditional way of raising start-up cash is to apply for a small business loan. One such source of funds is the Small Business Administration (SBA), which lends money to start-up companies. There are other loans for which you might qualify if you fit certain criteria, such as belonging to a minority population, being a military veteran, or having experienced hardship as a result of a natural disaster.

In recent years, the phenomenon of **micro-lending** has exploded. Micro-loans can be obtained from organizations such as Grameen USA or Kiva. Although these organizations originally focused on loaning money to people in the developing world, they are now increasing the services they provide to small entrepreneurs in the USA.

Acquaintances, clients, and members of your community are another source of small loans. Years ago, I had my hair cut by twin hairdressers who were trying to start their own salon. Eight of their clients, myself included, loaned them small amounts of money. In return, they offered us free hair cuts and a small percentage of interest on our loan. By doing this, they were able to obtain the funds they needed to start their salon. They were also able to pay us all back within two years. This method of borrowing can really work, and you would be surprised who might be interested in watching you cultivate a small food business. For many people, watching a small business grow is a reward in and of itself.

Crowdfunding is a relatively new phenomenon that allows you to approach a wider audience when seeking a micro-loan. Internet-based crowdfunding platforms, such as IndieGoGo or Kickstarter, allow individuals with creative ideas to set a fundraising goal and enlist "the crowd" in helping them reach that goal. There are three main crowdfunding models:

1 Donors, sponsors, or philanthropists contribute money to a project, but do not expect a financial return on their investment. They usually receive some token of appreciation, which could be something as small as a bumper sticker or as grand as having one of your recipes named in their honor.

2 Lenders who contribute funds will eventually need to be repaid, perhaps with interest (this is how my friends and I functioned with the twin hairdressers).

3 People invest in a project in exchange for equity, profit, or revenue sharing. Therefore, the value of their investment will depend on how well your business does.

Crowdfunding platforms often organize themselves around a project type, such as artistic productions, social projects, or disaster-relief efforts. One great thing about crowdfunding is that it's not just a way to raise money, but a way to market yourself, spread the word about your business, and get a sense of how people respond to your product.

Bartering with vendors is another way of cutting costs and minimizing debt as you start your business. Bartering goes way back in time and has always been considered a gentlemanly way to conduct business. For example, approach the copy shop where you designed and printed your business cards and ask if you can provide them with catering. Give it a try, for you have nothing to lose. Who knows what will happen—maybe the shop owner won't be able to barter her product, but will be impressed at your effort and moved to help you out in other ways. The next time someone comes into her shop to print wedding invitations, she may just ask them whether they need a caterer.

Bartering services must be reported as income. Keep records so you will remember to list such services on your taxes.

Keeping the Money You Make

As head of your finance department, you need to cultivate the skills of a good money manager. You will be making non-stop decisions regarding where to spend and where to save money. Think carefully, for no matter how exciting it will be to buy every gourmet product you see, your bank account will plummet quickly if you follow that route. Some investments, however, can be helpful and rewarding. Will your business grow faster if you buy a sign for the side of your car advertising your company? Maybe. It's up to your to know when and where to spend.

One major expense that I had to think long and hard about was my first commissary. It took years to save the money, and I only spent it when I felt that the business was growing well. At that point I knew that I would not be throwing it away on a business that was about to fold. I'd gained enough experience to predict the average seasonal sales for my company, and therefore had a sense of how much I could spend without putting myself or my family in financial jeopardy. When it came to outfitting the commissary, I saved money by purchasing used commercial refrigerators rather than investing in brand new ones.

Sure, it's pretty, but your job as CFO is to ask yourself: *Do you really* NEED *it?*

TO MARKET, TO MARKET WE GO

As the marketing and advertising director of your business, you are in charge of building your brand, effectively communicating with the public, and fostering awareness of your product.

As your company grows, you will determine how much of your budget to allot to marketing. I would suggest that at the start you use minimal money and maximum energy. Later, if you have the extra funds, you can put them toward a marketing budget. Get out there and spread the word! Be enthusiastic when talking about your company. Entice people by talking about your best events, such as those with memorable themes and unique menus. Make your stories fun to hear. Pass out your business card. Most importantly, be passionate and sincere!

Nowadays, advertising is conducted in all kinds of non-traditional ways. Think beyond magazines, billboards and local newspapers. Have you ever heard of "guerrilla marketing?" It is a system of marketing in which a product is promoted using creative, unconventional, and low-cost methods. One of the first places I witnessed guerrilla marketing was on the stall door of an obscure bathroom in NYC. The clever postcard pasted there served as an inexpensive, out-of-the-box form of advertising for a local clothing company.

Think about your own way to guer-  rilla market. I can't imagine anyone would turn down a sample of your best cupcake if you handed it out on a busy street corner. How can you make this even more effective? Use small labels bearing your business name to turn boring toothpicks into attention-grabbing flags. Wear an apron imprinted with your logo. Smile. Laugh. Be friendly!

Don't You Forget About Me

Satisfied customers are your greatest marketing source. Don't allow yourself to fall off your clients' radar! After you've completed a job for a client, continue to cultivate your relationship with them. Send an email to former clients telling them about a new recipe you are adding, or announcing a Spring Special. You want to be the first name that comes to mind when a client is asked for a catering recommendation. Most people enjoy giving a positive referral to a friend. It reflects on their good judgment and enables them to help the friend at the same time.

Should You Offer Free Lunch?

Offering to provide catering for a religious institution, school, or non-profit organization with which you are affiliated can be another way to gain some visibility. Just think wisely about this, as you will have to absorb the costs of ingredients and carve the time out of your busy schedule. If you go this route, make sure you are providing your best services. The group for which you are volunteering or the group that you are helping will be genuinely grateful for your food, but if it seems ordinary, the marketing benefits may be limited. In the long run, your goodwill should benefit both the organization and your company. Working for a reduced fee may be a generous thing to do, but if it's not ultimately valuable to your company, it may not be worth it.

Get Branded

Your brand needs to be clear and strong enough to stand out against the competition. Needless to say, that puts a lot of pressure on you as the marketing director. To dispel some anxiety, let's go over a few branding myths.

One, a brand image is not to be confused with a visual symbol. Success doesn't hinge on having a logo as recognizable as the Target bullseye or the Nike swoosh. Rather, your brand image is the set of emotional and sensory inputs that a person associates with *your* business. "Fast and convenient" is just as much a part of McDonalds' image as the Golden Arches; "morning ritual" is as integral to Starbucks' image as the color green and the mermaid icon. You get the idea.

Another misconception about branding is that a brand won't succeed unless a product is absolutely unique. In Chapter 4, where I outlined the steps toward starting your own catering business, Step 1 was "Find your niche." The word "niche," like "brand image," can be a little intimidating. Sometimes niches are easy to define. For example, if all your competitors have a six-hour event minimum, and your minimum is three hours, then your niche market consists of people looking to have short parties. But most of the time, it's not so simple. If you're one of three sandwich-serving food trucks parked near a college campus, then both you and the other two trucks are competing for business in the same niche. You need to distinguish your product in some way. Maybe you offer your sandwiches on gluten-free bread. Maybe you offer a "Sandwich of the Day" at a discounted price. Anything you can do to make yourself different is a step toward establishing your niche.

Social Media Savvy

Define: Facebook, LinkedIn, Twitter, Pinterest.

If these words make sense to you, then you're on your way. Use their platforms in whatever ways you feel comfortable—a lot, occasionally, or not at all. It's totally your choice. However, if you think your potential customers use social media, and you aren't yet accustomed to it, force yourself out of your comfort zone to give it a try. Figure out how social media tools work—ask friends to help you, take a course, read about it—and dive in!

Social media can be an inexpensive way to engage existing and potential customers. Other people can virtually do the marketing work for you. Their repeated posting, tweeting, or pinning about your company on Facebook, Twitter, or Pinterest can generate interest (then inquiries!) all on their own. But it's important to assess which, if any, platforms might be useful to you. **It is not necessary to participate in all of them.** If no one you know has time to read blogs, it would be a waste of time to set up a blog drawing attention to your business. It is wise to understand which social media platform will work best for you company as well as your clients.

OFFICE MANAGER

As Office Manager, you will need to set up a space and furnish it with the equipment and supplies necessary to start your business.

A short while back, office supply retailer Office Depot conducted a survey asking small businesses about their biggest "pain point." Was saving money or acquiring new customers the biggest challenge for these entrepreneurs? No! "Organizing my office" topped the list.

Whether your office is a designated corner of your living space or a box with a handle that you store in your car, you will need a system for organization that keeps your business matters under control. Here are a few tips:

1. Have a place for important items such as stamps, letterhead, calculator, stapler, etc., and put things back after you use them.

2. If you use a computer for any part of your business, back up your files!

Financial records, past menus, e-mails to and from clients: you don't want to lose any of this information due to a hard-drive malfunction.

3. Do not let stacks of paper pile up. Stay on top of your filing. If you're technologically savvy, or if you have very limited space, you may consider scanning documents and filing them electronically. But whether you use paper folders or electronic ones, there are a few categories you should definitively have:

Inquiries: After having a conversation with a potential client, record the key points discussed, making sure to write down any numbers you may have quoted. Also record what you and the client agreed would be the next step in the process. If you need to respond to the client by a certain time, put that on your calendar!

Didn't Work Out: This is a folder for clients you never hear from again. Perhaps they chose another caterer or felt your prices were too high. If they are polite enough to let you know they are using another caterer, wish them well and place their information in this folder. If they call you in the future, it will be useful to retrace what previously transpired.

Client Folders: For every client, create an individual folder where you collect all menus, correspondence, notes and receipts. The IRS requires you to hold onto your receipts for at least three years. If you are ever subject to a tax audit, you will need records to compose an accurate picture of your financial activity. The IRS accepts scanned receipts, so if you use a scanner to make digital copies of your receipts, you do not need to retain the paper originals.

HEAD OF THE LEGAL DEPARTMENT

In this role, which includes several different components, you must ensure that your company is functioning in accordance with the rules and regulations of local, state, and federal agencies.

Make Your Business Official

You will need to determine what your city or town requires in order to legally operate your business. In my town, for example, I have to register my company name annually in order to keep legal possession of the name.

Decide Upon Your Business Structure

What sort of structure will your business have? You can operate as a "sole proprietorship" and declare your earnings under your personal income taxes. Or, you may choose to form a corporation and file a separate tax return for your business. There are pros and cons to both legal structures. I would suggest reading about these online or in your local library. You might also wish to seek a quick consultation from a lawyer, the SBA, or a local "legal aid" group.

Get Intimate With the Health Department

As already stated, you will need to become very familiar with the health department's rules and regulations. You will want to make certain that your company does not risk being shut down for not following regulations. Can you imagine having a job for 100 guests scheduled for a Saturday evening, and on Friday getting a call from the local health department threatening to close you down over an issue? Don't let this happen to you!!! Be sure and do your homework so you can rest assured that your function will proceed smoothly and successfully.

Find A Legitimate Cooking Facility

The odds of being shut down by the health department hinge in great part on where you cook your food. Most likely, you will begin in the place where you are the most comfortable, i.e. your very own kitchen. Most cities and towns consider this illegal. However, this is a risk that many people take when first starting out as food entrepreneurs. It is important to note that you may be walking a fine line by doing this.

The loophole? In many states, you can bypass the need to use a approved kitchen by calling yourself a personal chef, chef du jour, or accomodator. A personal chef cannot deliver *cooked* food to a client, but he or she can bring food to a client's kitchen and cook it there. In other words, as a personal chef, you could do preparation off-site, in a non-licensed kitchen, as long as you do the actual cooking in the place where the food will eventually be eaten. This contrasts with a full-service off-premise caterer, who by definition does actual cooking (i.e. gets food to the point where it's ready to serve) off-site and then transports it to a location where it will be consumed. If you call yourself a personal chef, you can do the prepwork in your non-licensed kitchen, as long as you make the argument that the food was not ready to serve until you brought it to the site and finished cooking it.

SO WHERE CAN I COOK MY *fabulous food*?

When it comes to finding a licensed commercial kitchen, try a "less is more" approach. You don't need your own private commissary, at least not at the start. Spend some time on the internet looking for a shared kitchen space near you, You may find a restaurant owner who will happily "sublet" their kitchen to you a few mornings a week. If you live in a large city, you may be lucky enough to find a kitchen that's designed specifically for shared use. The purpose of such kitchens is to provide legal space for food entrepreneurs, and they're growing in popularity. In Boston, a non-profit organization called CropCircle Kitchens, Inc. bills itself as a "shared use kitchen commissary and culinary business incubator." Quite a few successful companies in town have had their origins there. In Dallas, HourKitchen strives to "provide entrepreneurs a service that is economically superior to building or leasing their own commercial facility." CulinaryIncubator.com is an online database of commercial kitchens targeted toward people looking for a commitment-free place to legally produce food products.

Purchase Insurance to Protect Yourself and Your Company

Your next duty is to make sure you are covered by correct insurance. Soon after I began to receive money for my catering, I looked into Catering Liability Insurance. I wasn't thrilled about this, for although I was working incredibly hard, I was barely making money on my catering, and I did not want to spend my small profit on insurance bills. Still, I knew I needed to protect myself and my family. I was surprised and relieved to find out that the cost of Catering Liability Insurance was very low. What's more, I was able to obtain the insurance immediately, even though I had not yet begun to work out of an official kitchen.

All caterers need a general standard liability policy, preferably one that covers up to one million dollars in damages per occurrence. A stan-

dard liability policy covers categories such as products, completed operations, bodily injury, and property damage. If you wish for additional
protection, you can purchase excess liability insurance, which will cover
you in the event of a claim that exceeds $1,000,000, or another sort of
catastrophic lost.

A few more notes about insurance:

• It is easier for catering companies to get insurance coverage if they
do not serve alcohol, since there are fewer liability issues involved. For
many years, my company did not carry liquor liability insurance. Therefore, at events where liquor was served, it was my responsibility to
make sure either that the client was protected by their own liability
insurance (such as a Homeowners Policy) or that the bartender hired
for the job came with his own "Liquor Liability" insurance.

• There are also Single Event liability policies that a client, event planner, or facility may purchase. As a caterer, you yourself cannot qualify
for one of these policies. However, if you do not have your own liability
insurance, you may suggest this possibility to your client.

• Once you hire staff you will need to educate yourself about the
need for Workmen's Compensation. Workmen's Comp covers you in
the event that one of your employees is injured on the job. Again,
surprisingly, this proved to be remarkably low-cost and uncomplicated.

Think you don't need insurance? You may be a careful and
conscientous caterer, but you'd be surprised how easily you can
inadvertently damage a venue. Years ago, I received a call from a
client who'd been thrilled when he waved me goodbye after the
job. Yet the following day, the client noticed nail marks all over
his kitchen floor. Understandably irate, he accused my company
of causing the damage. Much to my dismay, I looked at the shoes
I had worn to the job—a favorite pair—only to discover that
a little nail had started to wear through the sole of my shoe. I
had to apologize profusely and pay hundreds of dollars to have
his kitchen floor refinished. Luckily, my insurance reimbursed
me!

Make Sure You Are Paying The Required Taxes

As we briefly mentioned when discussing your Policy Sheet (see Page 106), sales tax requirements are governed by the state in which you run your business, and they vary state-by-state. As we talked about then, states have extensive and idiosyncratic requirements regarding what's taxable. Texas, for example, has defined a category of items that are given out with food and cannot be reused. Toothpicks, napkins, straws, cake boxes, hot-dog trays, and more: these are all tax-exempt.

You will need to keep excellent records on all taxes collected from your client and submit these to your governing state office. Begin this on day one of your first sale. Playing catch-up is no fun. If audited, you will have to pay back all of the taxes owed.

As a side note, **if you cater for a non-profit organization, a 501c3, or another tax-exempt group, you do not have to pay sales tax.** However, you must obtain a current copy of the organization's tax certificate and keep it in your files. If you are ever audited, this will provide proof of why you did not pay sales or meals tax on that particular job.

Acquire A Standard Client Contract

You may be head of your Legal Department, but this is something you need to outsource. Go to a lawyer and have them write up a template for a caterer-client contract. You'll only need to do this once. If in the future you need to make minor adjustments to the contract for a specific job, you'll most likely be able to do so on your own. When a lawyer crafts a solid framework for a contract, you can safely take care of the details.

The large amount of information presented in this chapter is testament to the complexity of being owner of a small food business. It will no doubt be overwhelming if you focus too much on the extent of your responsibilities. I know that had I stopped to consider just how many positions I filled in my company, I would have been paralyzed by the pressure. But luckily, I just went along, completing the tasks that seemed necessary to succeed. You will, too!

There's no escaping it: fritters are only good when they are fried at the last minute. Much of the preparation can be done ahead of time, but no more than 15 minutes should elapse between the time they leave the frying pan and the time the y enter your guests' mouths. I have a whole notebook of fritter recipes that I've collected over the years. Mix and match ingredients or use them as singular items with a yummy dipping sauce. One bite of fried food rarely hurt a soul at a party.

Chicken Corn Fritters with Lime Aioli Dipping Sauce

INGREDIENTS FOR FRITTERS:
1 cup fresh corn
1 cup cooked chicken,
   finely chopped
3 chopped scallions
1 egg, lightly beaten
½ cup milk
2 tbsp melted butter
½ tsp salt
cajun seasoning
1¾ cups all purpose flour
1 tsp baking powder
oil for deep frying

INGREDIENTS FOR SAUCE:
1 fresh lime, squeezed
½ cup mayo
Spices of your choice

Combine all wet ingredients in a bowl. Add the flour, seasonings and baking powder. Stir until mixed.

In a deep fryer or pot, drop batter by tablespoons into the hot oil. Try one first to see how it's working. Fry for about 3 minutes on each side or until golden brown.

Drain on paper towels and keep warm until ready to serve (which must be soon! that's the whole point).

For sauce, mix all ingredients together. Pour into your favorite dipping bowl and pass along with these scrumptuous hot fritters.

CHAPTER FOURTEEN
Planning and Shopping

THE ABILITY TO EFFICIENTLY PLAN YOUR JOBS AND
MANAGE YOUR TIME WILL HAVE AN IMPACT ON
BOTH YOUR PROFIT AND YOUR PEACE OF MIND.

. . . .

Planning is the key to success in any business, and the food business is no exception. Whether you run a coffee shop or sell a line of hot sauces to a local bodega, your profit is determined in part by how well you plan. While the information in this chapter may be most applicable to a Full-Service Off-Premise Caterer, there are a number of strategies discussed below that will be helpful no matter your area of expertise.

This is the time to step back and take a comprehensive view of the event. You cannot limit your planning to the ingredients. You cannot even limit your planning to the process of making your menu materialize from those ingredients. This is where all the *other* details come into play, from the size of your serving utensils to the color of your napkins. If your role in an event goes beyond cooking and serving the food and extends into areas such as rentals, décor, or alcohol, you'll have even more planning to do.

Every job requires a customized timeline. For example, if a job is booked two months in advance, you'll need to start planning right away. If a job is booked two years ahead of time, start working with around six months to go. Of course, you won't always have the luxury of planning as far in advance as you like, and some things just can't be planned ahead of time, especially when it comes to food availability. But when you *do* tackle the planning, everything to follow becomes easier. You build momentum with every piece of the puzzle that you complete. By the time you start cooking, you'll be ready to go full-steam ahead.

PLANNING THE BASICS

Planning What Food Ingredients You Need

At least a month ahead of a job, take a glance at the menu and start planning what you will need to make it happen. I have a ritual. Sitting down with a cup of coffee, I first print out a fresh copy of my menu. I go down it with recipes in hand, calculating the necessary quantity of each and every item. I cannot stress enough the importance of carefully considering every single item. It can be frustrating to be immersed in cooking during the week of the job, and to realize that I've forgotten to gather some ingredients for an item on the menu!

With respect to quantities of ingredients, **I err on the side of abundance**. Overestimating the quantity of food that I need for each item allows for cooking or measuring mistakes. It is a time-waster to have to stop in the middle of cooking because you didn't get enough beef, or because you burnt a batch of cheese quesadillas. Running to the store is a sure way to break the flow of cooking. If you have to make an emergency trip, it might be hard to pick up the pace right away when you return. Best to avoid these interruptions by making sure you have plenty of ingredients in the first place. You can always use the extra items for the next job you have. Or you can feed your family!

Once you have made your master list, organize and refine it in a way that makes sense to you. I categorize the items based on where I'll purchase them. My habit is to use different colored pens to indicate different stores. I go down my lists item by item and indicate where I will purchase each thing. I circle everything coming from one store in purple, everything coming from a second store in green, etc.

You can also organize your lists based on when you will purchase an item. Some purchases will need to be postponed until the day before or day of the job. You could write one list and color-code it to indicate what will be purchased on your main shopping day, what will be purchased two days before the job, etc. Or you could make a different list for each day. Just chose a method that will work for you. There is no right or wrong, just what suits you as a budding food entrepreneur!

Planning How Your Food Will Be Served and Eaten

In order to start making plans for elements like rental items or paper products, you'll need to know exactly how your food will be served and eaten. You and your client may have agreed months ago on a final menu, but now there's a whole new set of details to consider. How many people will be seated at each table? Will guests go up to a buffet table to get their food, or will be courses be plated and served? If there is a buffet table, where in the event space will it be located? If dinner is served as a plated course, will dessert be as well?

Think about how the food will be served. If the tables in the event space are to be ornately set, with a roll of bread at each place setting, you will need bread plates and perhaps butter knifes. If, on the other hand, there will be a large basket of rolls located in a sea of other items on a buffet table, then separate bread plates likely won't be required.

I've found that the best way to deal with so many variables is to go down the menu item by item. Start with one item, for example, an appetizer station featuring two varieties of soup, served in teacups. Think carefully about what dishes will be needed. Will guests request a cup of each type of soup? If they return for seconds, will they bring back their cup or expect a fresh one? If these are hot cups of soup, should

I often have a staff member double check my lists to make sure I haven't forgotten anything. An extra pair of eyes is always helpful!

you have saucers to place under them? When you've got that covered, go onto the next item. Let's say it's salad. Salad will be served buffet-style, at the same time as the main course and side dishes. Okay, so you don't need individual salad plates, but you do need a large enough serving piece to place the salad. Keep on going in this fashion until you've covered every item you will need.

Next, think about the equipment you will need to produce and showcase your menu. How are you going to keep the soup on that appetizer station hot? Will you need special equipment like griddles or blenders or deep-fryers? If so, do you need extension cords? Will you need chafers on your buffet table, and if so, do you have candles to place underneath? Do you need any additional ice chests or cooling cabinets? Coffee urns?

Now, give thought to any food and beverages for which you may not be responsible, i.e. the things not on your menu. If the client will be providing their own bartender and/or liquor, are you still responsible for providing the barware? If they are providing their own wedding cake, do they expect you to provide the serving plates and forks? These are the sort of details you'll need to go over with your client in order to make sure you're fulfilling her vision and not forgetting anything important.

Planning The Event Space

After you've given thought to everything that will be eaten or drunk at the party, it's time to create a floor plan. This, your map to the event, should show the location of each and every table and chair. Once you've got your list of the items needed to prepare and showcase your menu, plus a floor plan for the event, your plan is well underway.

Tips for a Successful Floor Plan

Think about the sequencing of the event. For example, will there be time between courses for you to clean the main buffet table and set up dessert on it, or do you need an additional table so that you can start setting up dessert while the main course buffet is still in use?

The less involvement you have with a part of an event, the easier it is to forget an item associated with it. Pay attention to things like a special table for gifts, a rolling table for a cake, or a place for entertainers to sit.

Often, an event site will require a floor plan to be sent to them a couple of weeks before the job. If so, make sure it is legible and very clearly marked.

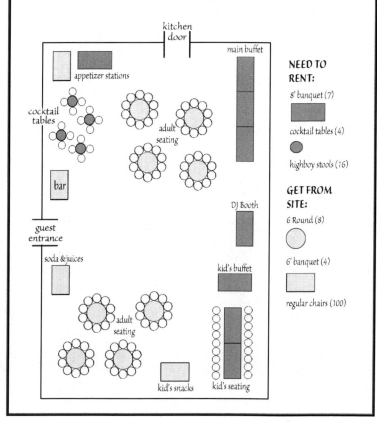

PLANNING BEYOND THE BASICS

Design and Décor

You may or may not be part of the décor and design for the party. If you are not, you will want the contact information for who is, and have a conversation with him/her. Obtain a sense of his/her plans regarding design concepts, theme, products, schedule and timing. You may need to coordinate your platters, presentations, napkins and tablecloths with the decorator's theme. Also coordinate your schedules in order to avoid confusion and chaos. What time does (s)he plan to arrive? Does (s)he need you to have the tablecloths down before (s)he begins to decorate the guest tables or buffets? Does (s)he plan to clean up the décor or is the expectation that your staff will take care of it at the end of the function? If the expectation that your staff will do this, where will the items be stored? Will the client take décor home or will the decorator pick it up at a later time? All these considerations work toward ensuring synchronicity with all aspects of the event.

If you are responsible for décor and design on a big job, begin forming a preliminary plan several months ahead. Create a list that breaks the décor needs down into categories: centerpieces, room design elements, lighting, props, and themed accessories. For each type of décor, make a list of the sources from which you will purchase your décor as well as the necessary timing for these purchases. If particular items will need to be ordered, find out how far in advance you need to place the order. Sometimes I have planned on using an item and ordered it with what I thought was plenty of time, only to find out it was out of stock. Oops! My whole plan had to be revised! Try to avoid this. Having a fabulous design is great, but unless you actually have the products in hand the day of the job, your job is not 100% done.

Overall, décor planning tends to require a lot of face-time with

Clash of the Centerpieces

Our company once did a job where we were in charge of the flowers on the buffet, while a floral designer had been hired to create the table centerpieces. However, we did not coordinator with the floral designer, and we arrived at the event site to find that the centerpieces were made of pale pink flowers and our buffet flowers were vibrant oranges and bold yellows! We did our best to try to make it work by touches of fabrics, but it was flawed at best. Thankfully our hostess and her guests were more focused on the celebration and food than the funky color schemes. It was a hard lesson learned!

clients. Clients tend to need attention and hand-holding with party decoration decisions. Try to keep an open line of communication with your client throughout the whole event process to help ensure that your client feels completely confident in your abilities to satisfy her design vision. Be open and available as you work with him/her in achieving a unified design.

Design and décor planning is an area you can wrap up early on in the process and put aside until closer to the event occurring. Everything you need to purchase can be ordered and/or received, your sample centerpiece can be made and shown, your room layout decided, and your special objects rented or purchased. Once all these pieces are ordered and in place, all you need to worry about is buying fresh flowers a couple days before the event.

Bar and Bartender

As bartenders can be in high demand during the busy season, secure one as soon as you have your date confirmed. Call six weeks in advance to reconfirm and make certain that they will honor the date. Even charming and affable bartenders can be human, too, and make mistakes in scheduling. This six week time period is especially important if you have to acquire liquor liability insurance, as that may take time to secure.

Another detail that should be confirmed six weeks before the job is your client's final decision regarding beverages. In addition to the alcohol needs for an event, consider what will non-alcoholic beverages will be needed. And don't forget ice! If you place an order for alcohol with a liquor store, check with the store a week ahead of the event date to make sure that the order is correct and scheduled for the proper delivery time. One quick call to confirm your order will alleviate stress for you. Another item crossed off well in advance of the job!

Special Items

When making a list of the product needs for a job, don't forget to include miscellaneous items such as cake candles, unique straws, decorative toothpicks, lobster bibs, or any other items you need to bring to the event. Make sure you put these items in a special place so that you do not forget them when packing for a job. Failure to remember one of these smaller items can be a big mistake in the eyes of your client and have a big impact of the success of the event. Candles, for example, are especially significant at a Bar/Bat Mitzvah lighting ceremony. Imagine forgetting those!

When you're ready to plan ... and they are not

Clients can and will stress over decisions regarding their event; and this is all the more true when the date is far on the horizon. "How am I supposed to know what I'm going to want my guests to eat two years from now?" they wonder. "What if my tastes change? What if our budget changes?" Decision-making may be difficult for your client, but the bottom line is, they need to make decisions in order for you to proceed with *your* work, and they need to make them on your schedule. If a client complains that it's way too soon for them to know their preferred table size or the number of bartenders they want, gently explain to them that while it is not your intent to rush them, it is necessary to adhere to time-frames set forth by industry vendors. Emphasize that the benefit of making these decisions early is that once these things are "signed and sealed", they'll be free to turn their attention elsewhere. Without overwhelming your client, communicate to them that before they know it, a new set of obligations will demand their time and energy. Without making your client feel like event planning is their burden —after all, they're paying *you* to do that for them—be clear about what you need. A request such as "If you can get me your seating plan by this week, I will take it from here," will result in your client completing their assignment willingly and on time.

PLANNING YOUR STAFF

Collaborating with a rental company, designing centerpieces, hiring a bartender: if you're the kind of caterer who doesn't offer these services, you may go your whole career without having to plan these elements. But everyone has to plan staff. There's no getting around that. You simply cannot complete a job without dedicated staff.

Having a cumulative staff list to which you can always refer will make staffing much easier. This list should include staff members' phone numbers, emails, mailing addresses, and availability. The more detail, the better. If someone has told you that they're often available last minute, mark that down! If you know that someone doesn't have a car and thus only likes to work local jobs, mark that down as well.

As you prepare a staff list for an upcoming job, look at your menu and think about your client. The menu and sequence of the event will guide you partway in knowing the necessary volume of staff. The client's preferences will also affect your staffing choices. If the client wants a four-star restaurant atmosphere, then try to use your most well-mannered, solicitous employees as floor staff. If she wants more of a fun ambiance, place your more gregarious or entertaining employees at the interactive stations. Bottom line: one staff member may be better suited for a particular client than another.

When I make my wish list of staff, I always start with my "core" staff. These are the employees whom I need at the event to guarantee success: my chef and my floor manager. Once I have these positions confirmed, I begin inviting other staff to fill in the kitchen and floor staff. Frequently the floor staff will be part of the kitchen staff and vice versa. However, I still start out with separate lists to see who is available.

As you receive confirmation or rejection of your staff's availability, adjust your next invite accordingly. If you have received a confirmation from three particularly strong staff members, you may not have to worry so much about the strength of the rest of the crew.

Make sure that you always conduct a preliminary check in with your chosen staff to determine availability for a particular event. There have been times when I've gone to staff a job only to find out that most of my staff will be out of town the weekend of the event. This is not uncommon on holiday weekends and school vacation weeks. Luckily, with enough time, I can scramble fast to find other sources for help.

As a final note, it is wise to think about having an extra staff or two come to the job just in case a last-minute cancellation takes place. Factors regarding staff not showing up are not in your control. An understaffed event is hard on everyone. The cost of backup can be a small price to pay to ensure that staff cancellations do not derail a big job.

ACQUIRING WHAT YOU NEED

You now have a comprehensive list of every item needed for your party, from forks to dessert plates to tablecloths to extension cords. The next question is: where are you going to get all this stuff?

More than likely, you'll get what you need from all over the place. First stop for shopping? Your own kitchen. Before you start shelling out money, know what you already own or have stocked. And as a corollary to that, never assume that you have anything on hand. If you will need salt for a soup recipe, don't leave it off your list just because it seems so obvious. When you're making a list of what you need, write it *all* down.

More likely than not, the food ingredients on your list will come from a variety of stores. Even for smaller jobs, I usually must go to at least five stores in order to get all I need. Of course, this is only practicable because I live in a large city. I can find almost everything I need in stock within a fifteen-mile radius. If you live in a smaller city or community, you may need to order your products well ahead of time or even place an order from the internet.

What about everything beyond the food? With luck, there will be some items that you can obtain without setting foot in a store or telephoning a rental company. Maybe the event is at the client's home, and he or she owns enough platters to serve passed appetizers. Make a note of that. Maybe your last job left you with a surfeit of blue plastic plates that go perfectly with the décor scheme for this upcoming job. You'll use them for dessert. One less thing you have to hunt down. Maybe the event is at a public space, like a community hall, and they can provide enough round tables for your seating. Mark that down.

Now where do you turn to get the things you're missing? Most everything can be acquired from a rental company. Even if all you need are two rectangular tables to supplement the round ones owned by that community hall, you can go to a rental company. At the other end of the spectrum, if you need enough fine china and linen to make a formal dinner for 100 guests, you can still go to the rental company.

If you start working on a list for the rental company far in advance of an event, you'll be dealing with estimated guest numbers rather than final figures. Even though you will likely need to adjust your order in the week preceding the event, your rental company will appreciate receiving an estimated rental list early on so they can begin their planning for the date of your party. If you initially tell the rental company that you need 75 six-inch white plates for your first course ravioli station, then small refinements, such as changing the number of plates to 82 or 71, won't cause a huge problem. No matter the final number of guests, it is wise to order 5 to 10 extra items beyond the "final" guest number. This will ensure that you have all you need for the event.

It's possible that, regardless of how thorough a selection your rental company offers, you won't be able to get everything you need from them. For example, say your client has requested a special chocolate fountain, one that your usual rental company does not have in their inventory. You could do research into finding a rental company that does carry the fountain, but this could take quite a bit of time and effort, and it would require you to form a relationship with a new vendor. You could suggest an alternative for your client, such as purchasing three small chocolate fountains instead of renting a single grand one. The cost might be comparable!

Speaking of purchasing things, there will definitely be situations where the best way to obtain an item is to buy it yourself. This will be especially true at the start of your business, as you aim to build a collection of items needed to produce your foods. If client after client ask for a chocolate fountain at their event, maybe your best bet is to purchase it yourself and recoup the cost (and then some) by renting it to them! If miniature macaroni and cheese cups are one of your specialties, and you keep seeing cute, well-priced sets of ramekins at a favorite store,

maybe it's time to stop serving your mac and cheese in flimsy muffin cups and start your own ramekin collection. You can add a small "Special Presentation" cost into your client's bill to help cover the charge.

TIPS FOR SHOPPING

The bad news: if you think of shopping as a relaxing activity best done online in your pajamas at 2 am, then shopping for your food business is going to be a whole new experience. The good news is there are ways to make your large-scale shopping less stressful. Here are a few:

one

The best time to begin your shopping is when you are fresh, energetic, and focused! You may be the type who does best first thing in the morning, when the birds are chirping and the dog is snoring. On the other hand, you may prefer to take care of your other duties first. Shopping may even feel like a treat once you have fed the kids, walked the dog, and paid the bills. Out you go with shopping list in hand!

two

It is imperative that you know store hours! Imagine going to a store for your items and finding it's closed on Mondays! And it's Monday! Stress. Frustration. Waste of time.

three

Think in advance about the items that will need to be refrigerated, and whether you will need to head back to your fridge on your route. Cold weather may buy you a little time, and you can also bring along ice chests to keep vulnerable foods safe. Still, it's more than likely that you won't be able to go the entire shopping day without returning to your refrigerator.

CHAPTER FIFTEEN
Cooking Your Menu

YOU UNDOUBTEDLY HAVE MORE COOKING WISDOM THAN
YOU REALIZE! NOW IT'S TIME TO GET INTO THE KITCHEN
AND PUT THAT TO USE.

. . . .

It is the week of the party! Excitement is in the air. Now you must add the smells, sights, and tastes as you proceed with the essence of catering...COOKING! After all, and after fourteen chapters, isn't this why you decided to give this great and satisfying career a try?

It is difficult to find textbooks or cooking resources with specific information on the actual act of cooking as a caterer. Many times, I've wished there were someone knowledgeable I could call or a text to which I could refer when I had a question or felt uncertain. How did this happen, when there appeared to be a surfeit of cooking information and cooking education at my fingertips? Couldn't I have learned these things at a cooking school?

Here's the truth: a cooking school will teach you how to cook in a commercial setting. They won't teach you how to pack up a 5-course meal for 50 and transport it from your commissary to a client's house, where you'll need to warm up those courses using just one oven and a small stovetop. These are the types of things a caterer needs to know. In this chapter, I'll share with you the handful of procedures that I eventually discovered for cooking *as a caterer*. Underlying most of these procedures are things I've talked about in other contexts: planning, organizing, creating systems that work for you. Hopefully, this advice will guide you through the cooking process, thereby increasing efficiency and decreasing exhaustion on those long cooking days ahead.

This chapter is not a place for me to tell you how to cook. I see food preparation as a process highly determined by an individual's cooking style. Whether you know if or not, you've already developed this. You have your own ideas of how you like your food to look, feel, and taste, and you have your own techniques for achieving that result. Don't devalue this, for it is what makes your cooking yours. If you've gotten the idea that there's a "right" or "better" way to cook, let that go. There's not a lot of consensus in cooking. Pose the same question to three chefs and you will hear three different opinions. Ultimately, though, the truth is that more than likely all three are correct, bringing their own style, expectations, and experiences to the table.

TIMING YOUR COOKING

In a perfect world, we would cook all our foods at the last minute, ensuring perfection. Alas, in reality, the catering world is far from perfect. It is not possible, even with an unlimited budget and numerous chefs, to cook all of your menu in one day. Your goal is to get as much food prepped and/or cooked ahead of time without compromising quality or safety. Planning, sequencing and managing will enable you to produce the safest, freshest, and finest food creations.

The ability to determine what you can prepare ahead of time and what has to wait until the last minute is the true ESSENCE OF CATERING.

When I was starting out, I pressured myself to do all my cooking as late as possible in the week of the job. This resulted in having to pull all-nighters or cook the day of the job, and needless to say, it stressed me out and exhausted me. As time went on, I became more confident that certain items did just fine when prepped or cooked ahead of time. In time, you too will come to intuitively know what can be done when.

You probably were very young when you figured out that if you slice an apple, it will begin to brown within a few minutes. And most likely, you later learned that lemon juice could preserve the freshness of a cut apple. Or maybe you're in the habit of waiting until your scrambled eggs are close to done before popping bread into the toaster. Guess what? You already have some knowledge of how to sequence your cooking. Trust what you've learned thus far. Expand your knowledge by working with another cook, observing and asking questions, or proceeding on your own with the trial and error approach.

Regardless of how much you know, questions, questions, and more questions will arise with each menu. Do you freeze risotto balls once you've made them and fry them frozen? Or do you make them, fry them, and then freeze them? The more information you gather, the wiser decisions you can make. Consult a trained chef, a friend who is a great cook, or even a detailed "how to" cookbook. Do not be fearful of experimenting. This is how we learn: a few steps forward and a couple steps back!

The Early Bird Catches the Worm?
Good Things Come to Those Who Wait?

Giving thought to the conflicting proverbs about timing makes you realize how much the answer to **when?** depends on context. This chart takes some popular food items and breaks up their preparation according to what you can do in advance, and what should wait.

	do it sooner	*do it later*
salad	Salad dressing can be made in advance. One or even 2 days before the job, you can chop crunchy greens like cabbage. Seal in baggies.	You want a fresh salad, not a broken down slaw, so wait until just before serving to "marry" your greens and your dressing.
proteins	The flavor of many meats is enhanced if they're marinated or rubbed a day or two before cooking.	On the other hand, if you marinate fish too far in advance, the texture will get mushy.
fruits	If necessary, you can take the skin off a melon the day before a job. Wrap it tightly in plastic wrap.	To avoid the fruit becoming too soft, wait until the day of the event to cut the fruit into small pieces.
veggies	You can cut, slice, and bag your veggies two or even three days before the job,	These veggies can be blanched the day of the job.
pasta	Pastas can be cooked three days ahead of time. Sauces can be cooked even earlier and stored.	Have a pasta bar at the event. Heat pasta in a skillet and add sauces as guests watch. Wow factor!

MULTI-TASKING

Cooking and prepping requires you to be efficient at multi-tasking. If you do not master this, you will be in the kitchen for long hours for days prior to the party. You will burn out and have no energy for the main performance coming up at week's end. Ever learned to juggle? Well, you're about to. Think through the different sorts of tasks you can accomplish simultaneously. While using the stove to heat water for pasta, roast vegetables in the oven. If you're baking a pasta casserole in the oven, start a sauce on the stove. If you're baking a casserole in the oven *and* using your stove to make sauce, start chopping vegetables for the next round of roasting.

If you have several recipes all it once, it is useful to take out and set up all the ingredients that you will need beforehand. This prevents slowing down and breaking up the flow as you work. Chasing down a particular seasoning or item in another part of your kitchen will be frustrating. In order to keep moving and producing, I like to think three or four items ahead on the menu. This keeps the process sharp.

As a **talented MULTI-TASKER**,
you'll bake, fry, measure, and clean all at once.
But there's one other task you must be doing
simultaneously: enjoying yourself. Catering is about
making people happy. If you feel wonderful about
what you are doing, your joy will be evident in the
taste of your food. Food is love. If you love the food
you cook, your guests will know it, taste it, and feel it.
Rationally it may not make sense for it is an intuitive,
spiritual essence from your heart and soul. If your
heart is not in it, ask yourself why not? Examine
this. A caterer should never feel that cooking is
a burden. It is and should be a true joy (at least
most of the time!)

Whenever a particular task is complete, I clean up my cooking space immediately. Some of my staff sees this as one of my "pet peeves." Their style may be to clean up at the very end of the cooking day or at less frequent intervals. For me, such an approach would lead to chaos. It's hard for me to imagine waiting until a recipe is complete to begin my cleanup, much less postponing cleaning until I've finished a whole day's worth of recipes. Taking those extra seconds to clean up between tasks is well worth it. It is easier to find the items, tools, or containers you are looking for, and it makes the end of day clean up much easier. Most importantly, it will save you energy, keep you well organized, and keep your food safe.

Not only should you keep your counters clean as you multi-task, but keep that sink clean as well! If I am cooking alone, I tend to clean the dishes, the pots, and the utensils as I finish with them. When I am cooking with others, I find it a must to do so. It contributes to less frustration between co-workers. It is easier for cooking staff to find items they need, and it creates a courteous and thoughtful ambiance in the kitchen. I recommend establishing a clean-as-you-go procedure as soon as possible with staff. Everyone will benefit from it!

PACKAGING

Putting food away and labeling it is a major component of all food businesses. In Chapter Eleven, we went over how to keep food safe once cooked. As you may recall, food can be safely kept on the counter for some time before refrigeration, and many foods *must* cool outside of the refrigerator. It's wise to designate an area of your kitchen to house your prepared food prior to "putting it to bed." If you do not have adequate space in your kitchen, you can use an inexpensive collapsible work table or even a desk surface to temporarily house your finished items. However, do not forget to take a break from cooking to transfer you food from this staging area into the fridge. I know that at times I get so far into the production of my menu that I come dangerously close to not putting my finished items away in safe time. Employ every method you can to remember this very important step! One suggestion is to set a timer to remind yourself to take a break and refrigerate your food, and then go back to your cooking.

Once you have prepared your food, it's time to package it. Again, there is no right way to do this. I have gone through different schools of thought about which way is best. I do like the large aluminum containers with the lids that many other caterers favor. They keep food steady and are easily stackable in your refrigerator. Using good strong plastic storage bags is another excellent storage method. These come in many sizes. With a few jumbo bags, you can put away enough pasta for fifty guests. With mini bags, you can store something as small as chopped herbs. There are other advantages of using plastic bags: they are relatively inexpensive, they're purchasable in a variety of places, and they take up little storage space. For things like sauces and dips, I like to use pint and quart size containers with fitted lids. These can be obtained from restaurant supply stores. Using recycled jars or containers re-purposed from purchased ingredients is another great technique. It's both environmentally friendly and low-cost.

*By **recycling and reusing** containers, you can find efficient, economical , and creative ways to package your products!*

LABELING

Label every item when you finish, no matter what! This will save you unnecessary stress and grief and will make your catering life so much happier. I promise! Use masking tape, packing labels, even pieces of paper! It doesn't matter what you use as long as the label is secured on. I cannot emphasize enough how important it is to label with the following information:

* the exact name of the food item
* the date it was prepared
* the date of the party
* the name of the party's host
* any other pertinent information that needs to be on that label

When labeling, use a waterproof pen such as a Sharpie. A label with rubbed-off ink is no good to anyone. Bring your labeling supplies to the job, so that you can label anything going back to your commissary and/or any leftovers.

READY, SET ... NOW WHAT?

No matter how prepared, organized, or exacting you are, something unexpected will likely occur at the very moment you pronounce your cooking complete. Isn't this Murphy's Law? Whatever can happen, will? But in the best case scenario, you'll still be able to finish up your cooking on the day before the party. At the point where none of your remaining To Dos can be tackled until the sun rises on Job Day, what should you do? If possible, nothing! Students are advised to stop studying 12 to 24 hours before a big exam. Likewise, your pre-event period should be a time for you to breathe, rejuvenate, and take a break from your work. Now is your time to make certain everything else is in place for the following day. Verify any arrangements you've made for your kids, your parents, your cat, your dog. Make sure your outfit is laid out for the morning. And, needless to say, get a good night's sleep!

On the day of the job, your physical, mental, and emotional state will be key to a successful outcome. Keep your schedule clear so that if any last minute crises do occur, you will be ready, willing and able to handle these curve balls. Yes, you may have to pick up some final items, or run a few unexpected errands, but if you have everything cooked, organized, and ready, you will be fine.

the way to start...

I love to cook, and I love my job as a caterer, but sometimes I get bogged down with "caterer's block." Julia Child probably had a case of it at some point. Probably Emeril as well. Why shouldn't I? Still, no excuse is valid when you have a job to pull off. As Nike says...."Just Do It!" Start with something you have done time and time again. Then go down that To Do list, and knock things off. In chef's language, prepping means actually getting an item completed, put away, and ready for utilization. Get your juices going! Find that as you stumble along, you begin to get a rhythm and to find your flow. Soon enough, you'll be enjoying the process.

...is by starting.

CHAPTER SIXTEEN
Packing Up

AS A CATERER, YOU ARE A TRAVELER GOING ON A TRIP. PACK YOUR SUITCASE WITH GREAT CARE. DOUBLE CHECK IT. IF YOU LEAVE SOMETHING BEHIND, IT WON'T BE EASY TO REPLACE.

. . . .

I've been catering successfully for many years, yet frequently do not sleep well the night before a job. I toss and turn and worry. Instead of counting sheep, I run through detail after detail, making sure that each aspect of the job is covered. At times I even bring the client's folder to bed with me and check my notes one last time. On several occasions, I've noticed something that I'd previously overlooked. It may seem unimaginable that something could be missed after so many reviews, but indeed, it happens. If it turns out that I need to attend to something first thing in the AM, I'll change my wedding ring from my left hand to my right, or write myself a big note and leave it on my nightstand.

Oversleeping is a big fear of mine, especially if a job begins at noon, or heaven forbid, earlier! Promptness is a critical factor in a successful catering job, so I usually set more than one alarm. Once awake, I pop up, hop in the shower, dress, and head off to pack the job.

Recently, I heard a tale of catering woe when chatting with a waiter in a local restaurant. Years previously, he had worked with a caterer, and one of their jobs took place on a little island only accessible by boat. The boss failed to thoroughly review his cargo after packing, and neglected to bring along several essentials for the job. There were no supermarkets in sight on this tiny island. The boss was frustrated, and the staff had to make do with what they brought. The goal of this chapter is to encourage you to pack as if you were catering a job on an island. There may be a supermarket right next to the event site, but pretend there isn't. Entertaining this mentality will encourage your packing to become systematic and streamlined.

PACKING IN THREE STAGES

Any packing system must be consistent and systematic, but aside from that, the specifics are up you. As you move toward developing a custom packing system, think about dividing the process into these three stages:

One	*Two*	*Three*
Assessing What You Need	Getting Things Ready To Go	Getting It All to the Job

ASSESSING WHAT YOU NEED

What Will You Need To Prepare The Menu?

A slow and methodic review of your menu is the best way to assess what you'll need to prepare it. Visualize how each item will look when served—and figure out what you will need to realize that final product.

The complexity of figuring out what you need to pack will vary. If there is a lot of variety to your business, each event will require customized packing. On the other hand, if your jobs are fairly standard and your menus narrowly focused, your packing will be more uniform.

What seasonings, garnishes, cooking equipment, or other ingredients are necessary? If, for instance, your menu features mushroom crostinis (heated on the client's stove), you will need: the mushrooms; a cutting board and knife for cutting the mushrooms; the crostini; the oil; a skillet; a utensil for cooking the mushrooms in the skillet; the appropriate seasonings such as salt, pepper, and garlic; garnishes; and a container to put the cooked mushrooms in before you put them atop the crostinis. All this for just one appetizer!

Needless to say, if you pack mushrooms and crostini toasts and oil and spices and garnishes, but forget your skillet and utensils, you're going to be in trouble. The "accessories" that go with an item are just as important as the ingredients. Often we overlook just how much stuff is needed to prepare or serve a recipe or its accompaniments. Charcoal for a barbecue. Propane for a stove. Colanders and a cheese grater for a kids pasta dish. A fresh pepper grinder for a plated salad. Squeeze bottles for chocolate and caramel sauces at a sundae bar. A carrot peeler to make spiraled garnishes. I could go on indefinitely, but you get the point: you truly have to consider the minute details of an item on your menu to make sure you've got everything covered.

Note how when I went over what was needed for the crostini, I included fundamentals like a cutting board, knife, and salt and pepepr. Pack your own basics thing even if it's likely that your hostess owns them: **you should not have to ask your hostess or your facility staff for anything!** I feel it is my responsibility to always bring the following: cutting boards, paper towels, trash bags, sheet pans, parchment paper, pot holders, toothpicks, knives, skewers, pens, paper for making food cards, scissors, can openers, corkscrews, aluminum foil, plastic wrap, serving utensils, leftover containers, and plastic bags. When it comes to this category of items, consider creating a standard packing list, one that you print out and refer to for each and every job.

What Will You Need to Serve the Menu?

Let me stress that the right serving utensils and dishes are critical to the success of your job. Imagine pieces of your precious lamb fillet falling to the floor because guests are trying to serve themselves with a pie server instead of a tong. Or think what a waste of time and energy it would be to replenish a dish every fifteen minutes because you don't have a bowl big enough to hold a larger supply.

A party's schedule, sequencing, and space should all be taken into account when choosing serving utensils, platters, bowls, etc. Consider how small nuances like the following affect what you will need to pack

- If staff will be passing appetizers, it's best to have a new tray ready to go each time the staff member loops back to the kitchen. This will require more trays than you'd need if you were to rinse and replenish each tray when the server returns to the kitchen, but it will enable the servers to return to the floor more quickly, which leads to happy guests.
- A larger buffet table may permit you to have a massive bowl of an item that you won't need to rotate, but if you have limited space on the buffet table, you'll need to use smaller bowl. Having a small dish on the buffet means you'll need a back-up ready in the kitchen, which in turn means you'll need at least two serving dishes.
- Think as well about the schedule and sequencing of the party. For example, if a buffet will be laid out for quite some time, at some point you may wish to transfer the foods into smaller serving dishes. This keeps the buffet from looking half-empty!

Finally, one tip with regards to serving pieces: Try to assign the appropriate piece(s) to every menu item ahead of time. You can even label serving pieces with masking tape to show what menu items they go with, or annotate a copy of your menu with descriptions of the utensils and dishes you plan to use.

What Will You Need to Serve Beverages?

If you're responsible for beverages for a job, your packing list expands exponentially. There are so many accessories needed! Have you got coffee, tea, sugar, sugar substitutes, cream, milk, half and half, honey and lemon, stirrers or spoons, signs indicating decaf, regular, and hot water? Enough seltzer and soda? Juices or flavored waters will require pitchers and garnishes and powdered mixes. Be careful, because your menu might omit the specifics of the beverages to be served, or it may not even mention them at all. As a result, it is easy to forget an element or two.

What Additional Items Will You Need?

We've talked a few times now (primarily in Chapter 8) about the possibility of taking on more than just food and service. If you have indeed purchased room décor, tablecloths, party favors, centerpieces, etc. for the event, these will need to be packed, of course. If the client has requested paper products, they will need to be packed as well! I make it a habit to throw in some extra napkins, utensils, and plates to assure me that we have plenty. If a package of napkins falls out when we're unloading, I have another package just in case. Use the old Girl (or Boy) Scout mantra: Be Prepared!

GETTING THINGS READY TO GO

Okay, so you've figured out what you need to bring to the job. You know what will be necessary to set up the site, prepare and serve your menu, and close down the job. The next step is finding a way to make sure that it all gets packed. You need an "out spot": a place where things "wait" until you load them into your vehicle.

One effective way of organizing (and this happens to be the way we do it at Miss Jeanies) is to use boxes or bins to group together the different components of each menu item. These kits allow you to put ingredients and other necessities into the fridge or onto the rack in a way that clearly signals "Take me!" For example, say you're doing a job with a guacamole bar. The day before the job, you prep the perishable vegetables—chopped tomatoes, onions, jalapeños, and cilantro—and make salsa. You package these in plastic containers or baggies and label them, then put those together in a large bin in the fridge. Into that bin you add a few quarts of sour cream. You'll then use another box as a kit for the items that don't require refrigeration: avocados, extra onions and tomatoes, limes, corn chips, maybe a jar of store-bought salsa (shhhhh). The non-refrigerated kit will also include your preparation equipment, such

Any packing system must be consistent and
systematic, but aside from that,
the specifics are up you.

as mortars and pestles, a lime squeezer, knives. When it comes time to load the van, you'll know that as long as these kits get into the trunk, you're all set for the guac bar. This bit of planning can save a lot of time.

I really recommend having each kit be exclusive to one menu item. If I'm using Parmesan cheese for both a Caesar salad and a butter-and-cheese ziti, for example, I'll separate the cheese and put the correct quantity in each kit. One advantage of this is that I can assess quantities better when things aren't combined, thus making sure I really am bringing enough. That said, I usually have at least one central kit full of "Greatest Hits" items, like spices, herbs, and oils.

Should you group your serving utensils and dishes with the corresponding kit for a menu item? If it makes sense to you to do so, then go ahead. Keep this in mind: let's say that the job with the Guacamole Bar features a Sundae Bar for dessert. You make a kit for the dry toppings: sprinkles, nuts, M&Ms, a jar of maraschino cherries. There's going to be a long break between courses at this party, and your plan is that after you shut down the guacamole bar, you'll wash the small mix-in bowls and serving spoons and then use those for the sprinkles, nuts, and maraschino cherries. But the bowls and serving spoons can't be in both kits at once. It can be helpful to place a note in the Sundae Kit— "Use bowls and spoons from Guac Bar." Otherwise, when you double-check your Sundae Kit, you might assume that you've forgotten to pack the bowls and spoons. Little notes can save you the aggravation of trying to pack something you've already packed away!

Even if you don't make kits in this fashion, I recommend finding another way to lay things out and group them. You might find it useful to make "loading zones." Use counters, tables, or corners to mark out designated areas for dry goods, paper products, platters, etc. When all is easy to view, your eye can scan quickly over the items to be packed, double-checking that you have all you need for the day. You're conducting a dress rehearsal, in a sense. This gives you the opportunity to notice and correct any mistakes that you've made. If you notice that you're short a sleeve of coffee cups or that one of your heads of lettuce is looking too brown, you have time to correct these mistakes. On the day of the job, this won't be the case.

Given how much I stressed the importance of lists in Chapter 14, you may be surprised that I haven't encouraged you to write out a packing list. While this is a system that works well for many, I find it too time consuming for my taste. Still, while spreadsheets and inventory logs aren't my style, they may be yours. If you go to this effort, bring a clean copy of the list to the job, so that you can make sure that everything that came with you goes back home!

GETTING IT ALL TO THE JOB

The road to success need not be traveled in an official catering vehicle! If you can afford a van that will transport all your catering items, that is wonderful. However, it is not a necessity. If you live in NYC, for example, you can always rent a van or large car to transport your goods. Make sure to factor the rental cost into your event budget. You can bill it as a "transportation fee." You could also try to arrange to borrow a vehicle from a family member or friend. Bartering is a third option. Your friend will loan you his truck if you promise to cater a dinner party for six of his closest buddies.

For years I have relied on my family's good old reliable minivan. By some spatial miracle, I always manage to fit in everything necessary. At times, I open the trunk and think, "No way will it all fit." And, alas, it does! Closing the sliding door is a magical moment. Every food item, every platter, every décor piece has a home in the family minivan! And off we go!

After all this effort, the last thing you need is to have any of your items damaged in transit. Here are some packing tips to minimize that possibility:

- Put more solid items, such as aluminum pans, on the bottom.

- Leave as little space between items as possible.

- Have the most delicate items sit beside you on the passenger seat, where you can keep an eye on them.

- If necessary, put precarious containers within larger containers. All it takes is one unexpected bump or one very sharp turn for a lid to fly off. If, heaven forbid, that lid was covering something like soup, that soup is about to splash all over the place.

Once on the road, I drive gingerly at first, aware that my catering loot is precious and needs to be transported carefully and safely to the destination. The first corner I turn is critical. I listen, praying that no glass has shattered, no box has fallen, and no food item has overturned! If I have packed cautiously and thoughtfully, I feel confident, after that first turn, that I can proceed without "too much" caution to my job site.

This is sounding like quite the obstacle course, isn't it? Well, here's the next threat to your smooth arrival: traffic delays! Say hello to our old friend, Murphy's Law. Nothing is worse than hitting unexpected traffic or roadwork and realizing you will be late for the job. What is a caterer to do? First of all, always leave yourself plenty of time to travel. Give yourself an extra thirty minutes to an hour to reach your destination. Secondly, before you leave the packing site, find out on the news or by any means possible if your route has traffic back up. If so, find other routes to take. A GPS, if at all possible, could be an invaluable investment. And if all else fails and it looks like you will be late, CALL THE HOSTESS. This is so important. He or she will be anxious, and you must do all you can to put him/her at ease. Clients can tolerate a short delay as long as they have been notified.

Just as you must do everything in your power to arrive on time, so must your staff. Make this expectation clear. The schedule does not allow for tardiness at all. If a staff member shows up 15 minutes late, it can throw everyone off. Staff needs to know that if they cannot be prompt, they cannot be on your staff. Once in awhile something occurs and a staff member may know he/she will be a few minutes late. You need to have a policy stating that all staff members must call you to let you know they will be late.

Onto the job!

Where will your catering take you?

CHAPTER SEVENTEEN
The Scene of the Party

TIME TO MOVE-IN AND SET UP. REMEMBER EVERY-
THING THAT WAS PUT OFF UNTIL THE LAST MINUTE?
WELCOME TO THE LAST MINUTE.

It is common knowledge that moving to a new home is one of the major stressors in life. Well, so is "moving in" to an event site. In this chapter, I'll share my hard earned lessons on how to make it smooth— or smoother.

Lesson One: you're not the only person stressed out about this move. Pay heed to the anxiety that an individual undoubtedly experiences when renting their facility to a new caterer. Whether they're the site owner, the custodian, or the event manager, they take great pride in their "home." It's up to you to earn their trust and bolster their confidence in you and your company. Be respectful and considerate of their property and, above all, comply with any and all rules they set forth. Instructions that may seem arbitrary at first likely stem from experiences that occurred over the years. And needless to say, following the site rules to a "T" is the best way to guarantee that you'll get back any security deposit you may have paid.

Before you start to unload, go into the site unencumbered and locate the "Point Person," i.e. the person in charge. A Point Person may be an event manager, a facility employee, a close relative or friend of your client, or the client herself. This is the person to whom you will turn if you need someone to make a call during the evening. Introduce yourself if necessary. If you have staff with you, introduce them. Tell the Point Person that you will be orienting yourself and the staff to the site, after which you will begin moving in. Although it is likely that you have already familiarized yourself with any special rules or requests, I recommend that you clarify expectations with the Point Person, just to make sure

you are both on the same page. Some pertinent questions include:
* Where should my staff and I park after unloading?
* Is it all right to keep an exit door open while unloading?
* Are there areas where food is not allowed?
* How should we handle trash?
* Should we be aware of any quirks related to the kitchen?
* Is there anything else of special importance we need to be aware of?
* If we need assistance at any point during the event, how can we contact you?

Calm is Contagious

From the moment you arrive on site, it is imperative that you remain calm. **Your mood greatly impacts that of those around you.** Quelling any anxiety that your client may have is part of your job, and trust me, your client *will* get anxious. Think of it from her perspective: four strangers walk into your lovely, clean home with arms full of boxes, crates, bins, buckets of flowers, fabrics, etc. All of a sudden your home sweet home looks like a hurricane hit. You have no idea that you're in capable hands, and that this mess is a necessary step in pulling together a fabulous event replete with glorious food and gorgeous presentation.

As the caterer, learn to "read" your client. If she seems anxious, immediately take a proactive stance by informing her that it may look chaotic but will be completely organized well before the first guest arrives. Reassure her. Hold her hand a bit. Explain how the process will unfold. **It's her party and she'll cry unless you stop her!**

At Miss Jeanies, our policy states that thirty minutes prior to the time that the event is to start, we drop whatever else we're doing in order to clean the front of the house and organize the kitchen. This alleviates much apprehension that the client may be feeling. Remember how badly she wants her party to be "perfect." It is a very special occasion, and she wants it all to flow smoothly.

A STRONG START

The first thirty minutes at a job are of paramount importance. As soon as you've oriented your core staff, you should proceed with unpacking. Begin by taking a few minutes to get organized: **if you arrange things systematically now, you can save valuable minutes later on.** Establish a holding location for each type of item, i.e. paper products in one spot, beverages in another, serving pieces yet somewhere else. Cooking equipment and cooking utensils should be placed near or on the stove. Make sure that all staff is oriented to this set-up. The larger the event and the more staff members you have, the more important it becomes that everyone is aware of the system.

Sometimes during a move, we are so eager to get started that we will quickly move things off a client's counter or table. At the end of the job, it can be hard to remember where an item was stashed. Make a note of where you put something, or tell a second person about the relocation; otherwise you'll waste valuable time at the end of the night.

In addition to unpacking, there are a couple of tasks that need to be done immediately after arrival at the site. Set up a washing station. You will need: soap, sponges, towels, paper towels, and trash bags. Many facilities do not provide these. In private homes, it is best to bring them

Has anyone seen the _____??
Do not panic if you left something back at your home or commissary. Calmly problem solve as best you can. There are numerous stories of caterers substituting one item for another when necessary. One time when we forgot to bring a can opener to a job, our lovely Caribbean chef quickly pried off the lid with a sharp instrument. She learned many such tricks growing up in Grenada. Necessity is definitely the mother of invention!

with you (See page 197). By the way, it works well if staff take turns washing dishes throughout the event. It's good for morale if no one person feels like *The* Dishwasher for the night!

Set up your trash system. For sanitation purposes as well as sanity, it is critical to stay on top of trash removal. If at all in doubt, find out from your Point Person where trash should go. Assign staff members to keep a watchful eye out for the trash and remove it ASAP before it gets too full (or worse, before it begins to attract flies or other insects, which can easily happen during a summertime event).

PREPPING FOOD ON SITE

Now that your kitchen is organized, it's time to begin preparing your food. Dozens of tasks must be completed before the menu is ready to serve. Make sure that your staff has a sense of how much time you have allocated to get each item done. Nothing will stress you more than having a staff work too slowly on a fruit bowl while there are thirty other tasks that need to be completed in an hour. It's a good idea to annotate your prep list with the estimated length each task should take. As staff move from task to task, they will be able to see how much time they have to get each one done.

What sort of preparations should come first? Some chefs prefer to begin with appetizers, others with food that will be served much later in the party. The important thing is to never assume that you'll have time later on to get something done. More than likely, something unexpected will occur that will pull you away from your stove. That's just how this business goes. You may need to pitch in on the floor, clean up a broken trash bag, or just catch your breath. This is why I advise you to get to the job early enough to prep your food at a steady pace. Leave yourself enough time so you don't get heart palpitations. Even if you lose a little money by spending more time on site than you budgeted, it's worth it. If you can make and follow a realistic cooking schedule, you'll feel secure regardless of how busy things get during the event.

There's one important rule of thumb for preparing your food on site: get it to a state where it can be held without losing quality or becoming unsafe, but will only require finishing touches in order to serve. You don't want to prep the food to a point where it will be wrecked if not served right away,

> **For all menu items, regardless of whether they'll be served hot or cold, the goal is the same:** *Bring the food as far along as possible without ultimately hurting the quality of the food.*

but you no longer have the time to put things off.

You can't get a head start on everything. If you begin cooking scallops in a skillet early on the day of a party, they'll taste like rubber. But most items are amenable to being prepped, at least in part, a few hours before serving. If your dessert includes a Design-Your-Own-Crêpe Bar with a variety of fruit toppings, and you slice the bananas early in the day, they'll be brown and unappealing by the time they're served. You might have to save the banana slicing until the last minute, but you *can* prepare and refrigerate the crêpe batter ahead of time. You can get your whipped cream ready. You can put your chocolate and caramel into squeeze bottles. You can even slice some fruits a couple hours in advance. Getting all this done early on is the best way to ensure that, at the last minute, you or a staff member will be free to start peeling and slicing bananas.

Here's another example: Tuna Tartar in Wonton Cups. Unless you put the tuna tartar in wonton cups at the last minute, the result will be mushy. However, you can accomplish part of the work early on: dice the fresh tuna, add spices, juice, oil, etc, place the mixture in a sealed container, and store it in the fridge. Wait until the appetizer period approaches until you start arranging wonton cups on a tray and filling them with the prepared tuna,

When it comes to foods that will be served hot, it's even more important to get an early start on cooking them. You most likely will not have the oven space to get everything done at the last minute! What's more, packing an oven with numerous items will slow down your cooking times. You may think you've allocated enough time to heat your rice dish, vegetables and chicken, but when the timer goes off, you find that the chicken is still cold inside. No good!

The same rule that we applied to cold dishes applies to hot ones: get them as far along as possible without compromising the quality or safety. For most cooked foods, this translates to cooking them about 95% of the way a few hours before serving time, then popping them back

Try Before You Fry (or Bake, or Broil)

Imagine putting a nearly-cooked risotto into the oven for a finishing round. You've paced your cooking well and you feel relaxed. But when you take out the risotto ten minutes later, you find that it has burnt! **No matter where you are, in a home or at a huge event site, remember to test out the ovens.** No matter what the site coordinator or the host may tell you, you never know if the stove cooks 100 degrees higher than normal. I can't tell you how many trays of burnt appetizers I've seen result from chefs not bothering to test an appetizer or two. If a whole pan of risotto gets scorched the day before the job, you'll lose some time and money, but you make a new batch. Not so if the dish is ruined five minutes before it needs to be served!

into the oven for five to ten minutes right before they'll be served. Some items will be cooked in two stages. With a macadamia-crusted fish, for example, we might begin cooking it on the morning of the job, get it about 95% of the way done, and finish it off at the last minute. Other items are cooked in three stages: with a chicken dish or a pork roast, we might actually start the cooking the day *before* the job. When we arrive at the site our chicken will already be 80% cooked, or our pork roast seasoned and seared. We will then bake the chicken or roast the pork until it's about 95% completed but not yet at the perfect doneness. And finally, right before serving, we'll very carefully give it a few more minutes of cooking time.

We use the same technique for cooking side dishes as we do for appetizers and entrées: we bring them as far along as we can without hurting the quality of the food. Pasta may be simple, but in the busy hours before a job, you certainly don't want to tie up a stove waiting for a four gallon pot of water to boil! So we precook the pasta the day before an event and take it off the stove while it's still *al dente*. When it is time to serve it, we warm it up and top it off with a sauce that we cooked the day before, sprinkle with some finely chopped herbs, and voilà—it tastes perfectly fresh!

I know that I threw around a lot of percentages in the preceding paragraphs! You're probably asking yourself how the heck you know when a chicken is 95% cooked. Many chefs don't go by temperatures when judging whether a dish is done: we just look, prod, and taste. But food safety guidelines decree that you use a food thermometer to ensure that meat, poultry, seafood, and other cooked foods reach a safe minimum internal temperature. What is considered safe varies from food to food: for example, chicken must have an internal temperature of 165°F, but lamb chops are safe at 145°F.

One important thing to note is that **even when rewarming something that was previously fully cooked, it must reach 165°F to truly be deemed safe.** Precooked foods that are merely "warmed" but not heated throughout are capable of causing food poisoning. Any sauces, soups, gravies, or other "wet" foods must be heated to a rolling boil before they are served. This means that the precooked tomato sauce that we used for our pasta in the above example must be brought back to an appropriate temperature before serving.

In the midst of all this food preparation, don't neglect your beverages. Drinks are a task that can be done early on. Non-alcoholic beverages such as lemonades, iced tea, and tap water with fruit slices can be made and refrigerated. And trust me, get a head start on your coffee. Coffee is the caterer's nemesis. Undoubtedly no matter what kind of coffee maker you're using, there will be a coffee issue. The pot will deliver hot water, weak coffee, coffee with grinds in it, or no coffee! We've discovered all kinds of tricks for coffee disasters, and we like to start troubleshooting early on.

THE FRONT OF THE HOUSE

An important way to help the client relax is to pay attention to setting up the front of the house. The client's priority at the event is usually where her party will take place, rather than her kitchen. The kitchen becomes the caterer's domain; whereas the party setting is the client's showplace.

One important reason to set up the front of the house first is to make certain that all critical rentals have arrived. Perhaps the rental company neglected to give you the correct number of guest table cloths. You would not be a "happy caterer" if you had a table for 10 guests with no tablecloth on it. Even the most fabulous food in the world could not compensate for that! Each guest should feel very special. If due to a shortage of rental items, one guest finds themselves with a dissimilar place setting, that guest will feel slighted. Call the rental company right away. If they're reputable and value your business, they will do whatever possible to remedy the shortage. The company we use has been absolutely extraordinary at delivering items either forgotten by us or them. I often joke that they seem to helicopter in our missing pieces. Keep in mind the time anticipated for the items to arrive. If you feel too much time has lapsed, call the company. Ask exactly what time they plan to arrive at the site. Assert yourself. Missing even one item can distract from the success of the party you have worked so diligently to create.

The Front of the House will really begin to come together once the guest tables are set. Once you have set the tables, move on to the décor. Place any centerpieces on the tables. If you're using other decorative objects, such as picture frames with table numbers, arrange those as well. If applicable, lay out favors and name cards at each place setting. When your table décor is placed and your guest tables set, you will feel an "ah" moment. The anticipation of knowing that your hours spent planning,

Forks on the left side of the plate, knives and spoons on the right. Water glass and wine glass are placed above the knives, with the water glass to the left of the wine glass.

Napkin placement adds a whole other level of opportunity for artistry. There are numerous creative folds for your napkins or fun ways to wrap them with ribbons or napkin holders. Napkins can be placed under the fork, in the water goblet, or in the "plate spot" (if plates will be picked up on the buffet).

cooking, and organizing will soon be coming to fruition is truly exciting.

Now it's time to organize the buffet tables as well as any stations. You will need to find an appropriate spot for every platter or bowl that will eventually be placed on the buffet, as well as for plates, utensils, and napkins (if utensils and napkins will be set up the guest tables, then only plates will be picked up at the buffet). Take the empty platters and bowls and set them down on the table to make sure they will fit nicely. Do not overcrowd the table. You want to give each item its own space. That said, you shouldn't arrange the buffet simply on the basis of aesthetics. There is a standard order for a dinner buffet: the salad, then the main entrée or two, then the carbohydrates, on to the veggies and finally the breads. This isn't to say that there is no flexibility or room for creativity here; after all, it would be equally logical to place the breads at the beginning of the buffet, to mimic the sequence of courses in a restaurant. The point is simply that dishes shouldn't be placed haphazardly at points on

Ways to Make a Statement on a Buffet:

Even if deep in conversation, guests will notice the first item encountered as they arrive at the beginning of the buffet table. Placing eating utensils in an eye-catching holder can set a stylistic tone for the party.

Add signage: you can display the entire menu at the beginning of the buffet, place cards with the names of individual items next to the dishes, or do both. Type up this information or have a staff member with nice handwriting write it out. You can also use signs to indicate special foods, such as vegetarian or non-dairy options.

Use unusual containers to hold some of your selections. A sombrero holding multi-colored tortilla chips will put a smile on your guests' faces! Rent a large silver pedestal bowl (the kind normally used to serve punch) to put your salad it. It will be unexpected and fun!

the buffet. Teaching your staff about proper food order, whatever you consider that to be, will save time and energy. In the past, I've made the mistake of assuming that a staff member knows my preferred sequence for setting up food on a buffet; being proven otherwise has led to a lot of frustration.

Once the buffet is staged, take a moment to look everything over. This is the last time you'll be on the floor before the guests arrive, so what you see in front of you is what they'll see upon entering. Refer to the floorplan for the party to make sure that all is in its proper place. Is the entire floor picked up and cleaned? Are all trash cans empty and all trash off the floor? Have you swept or (re)mopped the floor? If everything looks good, you can check yet another assignment off the list. Congratulations to you and your staff for spectacularly setting the stage for the event.

But wait, you're not *quite* done...

THE FINAL PREPARATIONS

The Front of the House is ready. Much of the food is set. Your host and hostess will soon make their appearance. Not only will they want to say hello, they will want to know that everything is under control. Stop what you are doing, even if you feel the crunch of time, and assure them that all is progressing beautifully and smoothly. Wish them a wonderful party.

With fifteen minutes left until the party begins, it's time to get your appetizers 100% ready. If you're passing trays of hot appetizers, think about how you wish to sequence them. You have a few options:

+ **The Assort-o-Tray:** Serve your full variety of hot appetizers from the start. While you'll be sacrificing the surprise of new appetizers, bringing out a multitude of appetizers right at the beginning of the party creates excitement. In terms of practicality, if you're going to pass a variety of appetizers at once, then you have to time it so that a variety of appetizers come out of the oven at once. I call this the "assort-o-tray" method. Put 6-8 of each type of appetizer on a parchment-lined tray and heat those up about 15 minutes before the event begins.

+ **The Single File:** Start by serving just one hot appetizer, waiting until it runs low, or until guests begin to turn it down, to bring out a second one. The benefit of this is that it doesn't "show your hand" as quick;y. Guests like the fact that there is always a new surprise coming.

+ **The Compromise:** Bring out most of your appetizers at the start, but hold one or two back for a half-time surprise.

As your hot appetizers sit in the oven, getting to that perfect temperature, you should do any last-minute prep work for your cold or room-temperature appetizers. If you were waiting until the last minute to top your cheddar biscuits with jalapeño jelly because they're so quick to get soggy, well, the last minute is here. As you assemble your passing trays, put a pretty flower or decorative garnish on each one. Also make sure that cocktail napkins are placed right next to the passing trays, so that floor staff can grab a handful each time they head to the floor. With cocktail napkins in hand, the passers stand by, ready to bring the flavor of the company to the entering crowd. Here we go!

Is this the end or the beginning?

When a member of the floor staff arrives at an event, they're anticipating a long, hard night of work. They know that the kitchen staff have already been on site for hours, but they may not know just how much **more** work has gone into the event to get to this point. From the perspective of the kitchen staff, the party is the homestretch. The hardest work is over. Weeks of menu planning, shopping, and prepping is completed. It's just the execution of the menu now.

In the first drafts of this book, I wrote sixteen chapters about everything that comes before the party, and then one brief section on the party itself. I didn't even notice this imbalance until I showed what I'd written to others. From the perspective of a guest, or even someone who works the floor at a party, the party is IT. And yet from the perspective of a chef or caterer, this is when things start winding down. Quite a difference, right?

It may be the final mile of the race, but for some caterers/ chefs, the party is the hardest part of the experience. The final production of the menu is very stressful for some. Personally, it made me anxious as heck. Yet I've worked with people who rose to their game at this time. One woman in particular got into an amazing Zen flow. She could be slow, spacey, and off her game... and then once the party started she became focused. Any trace of anxiety disappeared. Another chef was slow as molasses during prep all week, then at the job she was as calm as glass. She still looked totally disorganized, but she was a master of coordination and got all of the many many pieces of food out at the right time, be they hot, cold, or room temp.

The following chapter is about the party itself, and while it's a longer version than appeared in early drafts of this book, it may still seem quite brief to some readers. But to some extent, a party takes care of itself; that's why there's only so much I need to say on the topic. If you've planned and executed the event down to the final details, the party will go along like a well-oiled machine. It just moves and flows, happily and seemingly effortlessly. There's a hum and dance that repeatedly feels magical to me.

CHAPTER EIGHTEEN
Showtime

THE KITCHEN IS PREPPED.
THE APPETIZER TRAYS ARE READY TO GO.
CUE THE LIGHTS AND RAISE THE CURTAIN.

Our in-house event designer "Miss Deborah" likens catering to the theater. Why? Because catering combines drama, comedy, romance, and unfortunately, sometimes a little tragedy. All the theatrical elements are there; the rush before the show, the adrenaline flowing, the joy of creating culinary illusions, the design and décor, and an excited and hungry audience! You rehearse your lines, ready your costumes, and perfect your props. You may forget a line or two. You may have to improvise. Yet no matter what, the show must go on! The difference between these two mediums? In the theatre, if one performance is a bust, there is almost always a second chance to perfect your act. A repeat performance is usually just 24 hours away. In catering, on the other hand, you get one shot. That's all. If an event is a flop, then that event will always be a flop, regardless of your future successes.

A DREAM CAST

If a Miss Jeanies event were truly a theatrical performance, and you read the cast bios in the playbill, you'd know that our staff are not your typical "professional waiters." As mentioned earlier, my original staff were teachers at my sons' elementary school. Despite (or perhaps because of) their unusual backgrounds, my staff never needed to be told how to act. They intuitively knew how to behave, both with clients and guests and with each other. Our chefs and kitchen crew were not authoritarian and rigid. No one yelled or screamed at anyone. If criticism occurred among staff, it was communicated through a playful, accepting

way. We were a "catering family."

As years passed, I hired friends and then friends of friends to join in the fray. Hiring staff through word of mouth enabled me to find wonderful, capable, and friendly workers who propelled my business' success. But as my business grew and I began bringing friends of friends of friends into the mix, I found that some of these rookies needed a little "making-over." I eventually established some ground rules for staff in order to ensure consistent behavior and appearance. This Code of Conduct is less a way of disciplining staff and more a way of making it easy for staff to know what is expected of them. New employees actually appreciate a brief 101 on the company's standards; it saves them from worrying over whether they're doing this and that correctly or not. A dress code is a must for staff. Our brand is characterized by a staff of well-groomed and well-mannered facilitators. Female staff dress head-to-toe in stylish and elegant black, though they're permitted to customized the look with accessories or other bits of personal flair. Male staff wear black dress pants and white or light blue dress shirts with a tie. We wear comfortable yet fashionable shoes; no high heels or sneakers are allowed. If staff have any body piercings, they must take out their jewelry while at an event (earrings are the exception).

There have been times when I've had to suggest to staff that they comb their hair or put on lipstick before going out onto the floor. This is understandably tricky, because I don't want to insinuate something insulting about a person's appearance. However, it is my job to make sure that staff look appealing for the hostess and the guests.

Of course, staff can't just look good; they need to act that way! Floor staff are under constant observation by guests, whether they're aware of it or not. The moods and attitudes of the caterer and floor staff are contagious; guests "see" and "feel" our vibes. If we are calm, happy, and relaxed, the guests follow suit. It allows the guests to take it easy, to sit back and enjoy the ride. It is vital that floor staff are upbeat, knowledgeable, and confident. Staff should be friendly but not overly talkative (It can be so difficult to stop yourself from participating when you hear a fascinating conversation between guests on the floor, but it's a must!)

One surefire way to keep bad moods at bay and staff morale high is to make sure that the scut work is distributed equally between staff. It is best to make sure that no one staff feels like **the** dishwasher for the night! Have staff take turns at the sink. There will inevitably be disagreements or clashes of personality between staff, but these can be resolved more easily in an atmosphere of equality and mutual respect.

A DREAM AUDIENCE?

Us caterers don't think a lot about the actual guests' experience while at the party. As a matter of fact, when I originally wrote this chapter, I didn't even give much thought to the guests. Only upon reading what I'd written did I come to realize that I was overlooking something.

A guest's state of mind is highly contingent both on the context of the party and on their personal circumstances. We think of celebrations as just that: celebrations. Guests should be happy, right? Well, the fact of the matter is that your guests may be employees drudgingly attending a birthday party for a boss they all dislike, or a group of protective friends ambivalently celebrating a marriage they don't expect to last, or nervous parents who've left their infant with a new babysitter. Is it your responsibility to ensure that everyone has a good time? No. It is your responsibility, however, to make sure you and your staff provide the best possible experience for all guests, no matter what.

Does this sound overly cynical? Perhaps. Plenty of

The best question for a guest to ask?

Who's the Caterer?

When a guest compliments your company and asks for a business card, take the request seriously and get a card to them ASAP.

guests are gracious and low-maintenance, but there are always exceptions. For example, you'll inevitably have to deal with the type of guest
who we'll call "The Interferer." This guest wanders into the kitchen
with a request they consider simple. "Just plain bottled water! Don't you
have that??" "Can you just make my kid a peanut butter sandwich? He
doesn't need anything fancy."

Another guest type, "The Information Seeker," WILL ask what's in
the food, where's the bathroom, how long 'til dinner, what's for dessert?
It's important to answer their questions to the best of your ability. Then
there are those questions that you can't answer: Is my car going to get
towed? Exactly how many ounces of sodium are in this pasta? Like The
Interferer, the Information Seeker is a pain in the neck, but if you want
good reviews, you need to accommodate them sweetly and graciously.

Questions regarding food allergies and other special dietary requirements must be taken very seriously. If a member of the floor staff
is asked a question about ingredients that she cannot answer, she should
bring out the chef to talk to the guest, or bring the guest into the kitch-
en. This level of scrupulousness will impress the guest. On a side note,
if you serve foods with common allergens, it's a good idea to reference
those allergens in the names of the dishes. If a passer asks a guest "Can I
offer you a Peanut-Marinade Chicken Satay?" (as opposed to just "Can I
offer you a Chicken Satay?") they'll stave off quite a few "Does this have
nuts in it?" inquiries.

In an ideal world, guests with severe food allergies would alert the

How to Answer Questions Like a Pro

when you have a free staff member: go the extra mile	when you don't have an answer: divert or deflect	whenever you can: promote and hype your product
If a staff member has a second to spare and wants to pull out their smartphone and look up whether cars get towed on that street, then by all means, go the extra mile. Just don't do this at the expense of other duties.	"I'm not exactly sure how many ounces of sodium are in the pasta, but I can tell you that we used very little salt in preparing the couscous!" With any luck, they'll go fill their plate with that and leave you alone.	"Here's some water, and I'm sorry that the bar ran out of diet soda. When we cater events where we're responsible for the beverages, we always keep plenty of that in stock! It's my favor-ite—well, next to our custom smoothies!"

hostess to their restricted diet ahead of time, or even bring their own meal with them. Unfortunately, this doesn't always happen. With a little spin, however, you can turn an "there's no food for you here" apology into a display of concern and flexibility. "You're allergic to garlic? You know, we really didn't cook with that in mind." If we're told ahead of time, we're totally delighted to accomodate special diets." For extra impact, point out an accomodation you've made for another guest. "See, we prepared these spring rolls without soy sauce especially for a guest with an allergy." And with that, point to plate of spring rolls! (Seriously, though, it *can* be helpful to have a few simply-prepared options available. Leave a small amount of salad undressed, set aside a few plain chicken breasts, leave the icing off a cupcake or two. If a guest shows up at the kitchen door moaning, "Isn't there ANYTHING I can eat?" and you have something on hand to appease them, their subsequent delight will surely garner you a good review.)

For the most part, guests don't want to know what's going on behind the scenes. But if an obvious mistake occurs—a glass drops, or a chair tips over—don't pretend that it's not happening. Though guests will stop for a minute, all you need to say is "We've got it," or "It's all under control" and they will resume their chatter.

A PARTY IN FIVE ACTS

Act One: (H)Appy Hour

The opening act of the show is almost always a cocktail period. A few guests arrive a bit early. One of your staff should welcome the early birds, show them where the bar is located, and offer to take their coats if need be. Often, those who arrive first are a bit awkward and unsure what to do. You want to make guests comfortable and ease them into the event. If a member of your staff is especially skilled at this, make sure they're assigned the job. If you're working alone or with only one or two staff, you'll need to be mindful of what is going on in the kitchen at the same time that you greet and orient guests. Once again, multi-tasking is the name of the game.

A successful appetizer period must be carefully timed. Rarely do people eat the moment they have arrived. They tend to feel over-whelmed if bombarded by servers while they're still getting their bearings. Usually the guests head to the bar first, and warm up with a few sips of alcohol. They'll check out the other guests, say a few hellos, and start gearing up for the party. If you read the crowd, you will know when it is time to start passing. Within five to ten minutes of arrivals, we will likely send the first passers onto the floor, but others will hang back until later in the hour. It is not wise to overwhelm your guests. If you go slowly, then like magic, the room will fill up with a critical mass, and all your servers will be passing appetizers happily and graciously, making frequent trips to the kitchen to replenish their trays.

I love the merriment of an appetizer period. It has a tune like no other part of the party. You can feel the pace quickening, the noise escalating, the rapidity of food consumption rising. There is a glow and a joy in the room. There's laughter, chatting, hugging, eating, and drinking. Your client can feel her vision of the event coming into being, and you feel all your hard work coming to fruition.

At the height of an appetizer period, staff make frequent trips to the kitchen, their passing trays wiped clean. But eventually they'll start returning with a leftover item or two on their trays. "Should we keep passing?" they ask. I tell servers to keep going. I think it's important to keep a presence on the floor, even when consumption is slowing down. As things slow, staff may alternate rounds of passing with rounds of busing the floor (cleaning up stray cocktail napkins, wine glasses, plates, etc.) This is very important: no matter what the budget, staff has to keep the floor immaculately clean. As they serve, they need to also look out for the wine glass that's been left on a windowsill, the cocktail napkin crumpled on the floor, the jacket that slid off the back of a chair. Your client will be pleased to see staff cleaning as they go.

At this point, there is still a lot of coordinating to do in the kitchen, especially if you have just one or two stoves. Even if you're still heating up appetizers, you'll need to readistribute some oven space in order to begin heating the main entree(s). Now is also the time to finalize the first course, if there will be one. Toss the salad with dressing, double-check the seasoning in the soup, do a final stirring of your sauces, etc.

Act Two: Please Take Your Seats

It's rare to have an event without some sort of break between the appetizer period and the first course, but it does happen. There isn't always the time (or the desire) to linger between courses. Sometimes the food is just a stop on the way to the main attraction of the evening, be it a silent auction or a religious ceremony. But more commonly, there is a 20 to 30 minute pause between the appetizer period and dinner, during which guests transition from the cocktail area to the main seating. This is usually when an emcee, DJ, or even the hosts themselves get up in front of the crowd and start "doing their thing." Coordinate the actual serving of the food with this action. The food should be plated and ready to come out as soon as the music or speeches stop. If you anticipate any difficulty here, talk to the DJ beforehand. He or she can buy you time by playing a few extra minutes of music.

Only once in Miss Jeanies history did we have an uncomfortably long lag between appetizers and dinner. This was a result of an old stove that refused to heat up our fish entrée in a timely manner. The crowd got restless. In retrospect, I would have had staff pass another appetizer to our seated guests, which would have given us an opportunity to assure guests that the meal would be coming soon. People are very forgiving when they understand what is occurring, and a few words of explanation go a long way. The lesson? It is a good idea to bring along something to serve the guests if an emergency appeasement is needed.

When should staff begin to clear the first course plates? Some etiquette books suggest waiting until all guests at a single table are finished

Beyond Soup and Salad

A successful first course can be any treat that encourages guests to sit and spend a few minutes chatting with their tablemates. As guests pass the platter of small breads and spicy hummuses between themselves, they get more comfortable. As they investigate an unexpected and unusual edible centerpiece, conversations spark. Clever first courses can reflect your creativity and artistic expression.

eating before picking up any plates at all. Others say it is fine to pick up plates as guests appear to finish, suggesting it gives an appearance of poor service if the plates are not picked up right away. The method you choose will likely depend on your client's formality or informality Remind staff to always ask the guests if they are finished before removing their plate. It is common courtesy to do so.

Act Three: The Main Course

Time for the main course, which will either be plated or served on a buffet table. If the meal is being served buffet style, a staff member should definitely stand behind hard-to-serve or difficult-to-understand items. If you have staff to spare, you *can* have a staff member standing behind each item, quietly serving. One key responsibility of buffet staff is to portion out the food in an appropriate manner. If guests help themselves, you may run out of food for those toward the end of the line. If you do run low on an item, put some tricks of the trade to use. For one, start serving smaller portions. Move anything that's running low to the end of the buffet, and transfer it into a smaller bowl or platter. Also, exchange the original serving utensil for a smaller one. Finally, before you run out

> **TIP:**
> If you can't have a staff member standing behind every buffet item, then just position a person at the most significant items, such as entrees or Wow! dishes.

of anything, put some aside for for your client. The host and hostess are often latecomers to the buffet, and it would be woeful if they missed the opportunity to taste the food they chose (and paid for)!

If you are plating your main course, the kitchen must have an organized system for getting food out as efficiently as possible. Plating works like an assembly line. One kitchen staff places the entree on the plate, another adds the side dishes. The floor staff, each of whom is likely assigned a table or two to service, takes the completed plates from the kitchen onto the floor. They will continue to travel back and forth to the kitchen until each of their guests have been served.

Act Four: Sweets to the Sweet

When all buffet tables are cleared of the main course, you can ready them for dessert. Even if you're not going to bring out dessert right away, get the tables clean. You may want to bring along an extra cloth or two in case any tables look a bit worse for the wear post-dinner.

Since you have already prepared as much of the dessert as possible at the beginning of the job, you should be in good shape to get it out. You should also have set up the coffee and its accoutrements in advance.

When preparing your post-dinner beverages, be sure to label pitchers or dispensers so guests can distinguish between regular coffee, decaf coffee, and hot water. You can also indicate what's half and half, what's whole milk, and what's skim.

NO *meal* IS COMPLETE WITHOUT *dessert*...
and no dessert buffet is complete without ...

+ the correct plates, napkins, and utensils
+ spoons and coffee stirrers
+ a place for guests to leave dirty utensils
+ any signage that identifies your desserts
+ a staff person standing by to aid guests and keep things tidy and assist guests as needed

---

The nice thing about dessert is that it's pretty much a guarantee that everyone is going to love it. People are less critical of dessert than they are of other courses. As long as it tastes satisfying, you'll get nary a complaint. It doesn't hurt that guests may be a little tipsy by this point. Give them a few dozen grams of sugar and they'll be quite content.

As for you...you're starting to feel the need for a little sugar and coffee. Your feet are tired. After four acts, this is normal. We've got one act left to go: rally yourself and get ready for the grand finale!

"STAND BACK AND LET THE PROS DO THE WORK"

Though a theatrical producer fronts the money for a performance, they often have zero hands-on involvement in the production. In this analogy, your client is the producer. Ideally, he or she will say hello and then leave you alone until the last guest has departed. I'd say 75% of hostesses are like this. The remainder, however, do micromanage. They'll come into the kitchen and announce "The janitor left a mop in the bathroom, can one of your staff go move it?" They'll pull you aside to ask "When is the salad coming out?" Some may become less vigilant as the party goes on, eventually losing themselves in the flow, but others watch and worry throughout the whole event. As with so much else in life, worry can become a self-fulfilling prophecy. If a hostess is looking for something wrong, she'll find something. We've only had a few "disasters" in the history of our company, and half of those have been at the parties we've catered for the hyper-watchful hostesses.

Act Five: Exit, Stage Left.

As the event winds down and the mood relaxes, you need to do exactly the opposite, for Act Five is possibly the most important act of the whole play. If you let your hair down at this point and fail to end this event in the most responsible way imaginable, you could easily wipe out the year (or more) of work you put into this job. Yes, it is time for another Miss Jeanies tale of "Oh No!" Once, my staff accidentally took a coffeepot from an event site. The site manager, aghast to find this "precious" object missing, insinuated that we had "taken" it. In a panic, we searched everywhere for the pot. Though we were able to locate and return it, the whole saga was traumatic and left a bad taste (pun intended) in the site manager's mouth. It made her judge us as careless. One small mistake for a staff, one giant mistake for the caterer. Need another example of the critical importance of wrapping things up carefully? Our designer Miss Deb was once given a very special silver bowl to use at a client's event. It was a family heirloom, and we tried to treat it as such. But sure enough, when it came time to return the bowl to the hostess, it was nowhere to be found. Needless to say, Miss Deb was in very hot water. Though she tried to make amends, no amount of apologies or money could repair the loss of such a sentimental object. We learned a hard lesson that day. From that point forward, we've always told clients that we can not be held responsible for any personal item that they loan to us. We try to dissuade them from using objects that are irreplaceable.

Clean-up is like leading the troops into battle. Everyone is exhausted, and yet there is much to be done before considering "calling it a night." Our motto is to leave it cleaner than you found it! If we had a second motto, it would be "cleaning is not a one-size-fits-all job." Pay attention. One time a staff member used books from a client's bookshelf to create height on the buffet table. She covered the books with cloth to protect them, but neglected to put them back on the correct shelf after using them. Though the house might have looked spotless to an outsider, it wasn't left according to the client's preference.

Along these same lines, most event sites have their own particular specifications regarding cleaning. For example, some might require you to pick up trash off the floor but not sweep; others might require you to sweep but not mop. Some sites will have dishwashing machines that you can use, while others will require you to wash dishes by hand. If you adhere very closely to the site's rules, you will almost certainly collect your deposit and strengthen your reputation. You should have received these directions when you first checked in with the site manager or point person (or even when you made a preliminary site visit), but if you have any more questions, do not hesitate to ask.

For an event at a client's home, the task list may differ slightly. Put all chairs back. Replace books, photos, etc. that were moved off coffee tables. Make sure there are no wet spots on surfaces where guests may have placed their drinks. Run the garbage disposal one last time, making sure there are no utensils in the disposal before turning it on. Wipe down the sink. Dry and put away any dishes in the drying rack. Leave the scene spotless.

> Despite your best efforts to pack up carefully, you may get a call in the day or two following the party asking if you or your staff accidentally took off with a belonging or piece of equipment. If this occurs, graciously offer to search for the missing item, reassuring the client that you will certainly do all you can to resolve the issue. If an item does turn up, return it right away, as clients may interpret a delay here as a lack of concern on your part. If the item is not found, it is wise to offer to reimburse the client, even if your policy sheet clearly states that your company is not responsible in such a situation. This is a difficult issue that should be dealt with on a case-by-case basis. Use your good judgment when deciding how far to go here.
>
> On this note, it's wise to have an internal policy regarding staff errors. For example, some companies dictate that if a staff members breaks an item, the staff member is responsible for half the replacement cost. Others implement a "three strikes" rule. Whatever the specifics of your policy, the important thing is to address these situations in a consistent way that assures staff they are being treated fairly and equally.

Hold on just a moment before you rid that kitchen of every needless crumb, it's critical that you pack up some leftovers for the clients. We went over leftovers in our discussion of Policy Sheets (see Page 108). As you will recall, leftovers are tricky, and different clients will have different wishes with regards to them. Some clients will see a table full of leftover kabobs and think that I purposefully sold them far more than they needed. I have a prepared speech that I give if they confront me with this. "As I told you in our first meeting, there are always going to be some leftovers. it's impossible to predict exactly how much a crowd will eat. We did a job last weekend, same menu, same number of people, and there were zero kabobs left! There's nothing worse than running out of food, and so yes, I do buy and prepare extras. But even if I'm buying 115% of what you need, just to be safe, I only charge you for

100%. So when food goes uneaten, I'm the one who loses money, not you. Could I have made a more conservative estimate of how much food your guests would eat? Perhaps, but I'm just not comfortable cutting things that close." I leave it at that.

Then you have the clients who see a table full of leftovers and expect you to pack up every last morsel for them. Hand these clients just a small amount of leftovers and they'll think you've stashed the rest away for yourself. In this case, the best thing to say is "We needed to throw away the food that was no longer safe to eat. We used our discretion in deciding what was safe to give to you."

Regardless of how much food you leave with the client, it's important to package your leftovers nicely. Put them in professional-looking containers such as aluminum pans or ziploc baggies. You can even create labels with your company's name and logo and use them to label leftovers. If the event is being held away from the client's home, be sure to

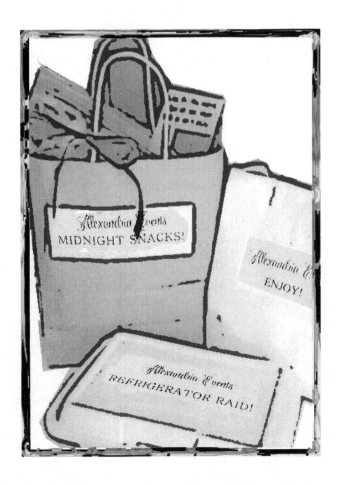

offer to carry the leftovers to her car. or possibly deliver them.

Are we done yet? Nope. Remember unloading the van seven or eight hours ago? Well, now it is time to load it back up and return to the commissary. This is a tiring endeavor, but not as tension producing as when you first unloaded. As exhausted as you are, this is not a time to be sloppy. Explain to your staff the value of careful and precise packing. I have watched helplessly as some of my most beautiful bowls and platters crashed to the ground after having been carelessly placed in the van. Profits lost from careless mistakes are painful ones. Believe me. The same precision is necessary when the closers unpack at the commissary. Even if staff is still being paid, they are exhausted and ready to go home—can you blame them? Still, it is tremendously frustrating to find equipment returned to the wrong places and perishable items left out. If you are not going to be at the commissary to supervise the close up, assign someone to be in charge. Let that person know your expectations. Don't assume they know where to put things. What is obvious to you, may not be obvious to them, particularly late at night after a long day of work. It does help if your commissary is organized in a way that makes it as obvious as possible where things belong. That said, while we have labeled areas in ours, it is still nearly impossible to get staff to put items in the correct place.

GOODBYE ISN'T FOREVER

One of the most important closing tasks at a job is saying a proper goodbye to your client. You want to preserve your relationship with them so that they'll call you again! As you part ways, let your client know that you'll be in touch. Present them with a care package of leftovers. If you want to receive payment from your client then and there, have the bill ready. Don't make them wait.

Everything is clean and put away. Staff has signed out. You said good night to your thrilled clients! You did it! You are so proud of yourself and your staff. You are exhausted. You have visions of getting home, flopping into bed, and falling asleep. Dream on! It's not going to happen. Instead you're filled with extra energy and your head is swimming with thoughts. After many jobs, despite being nearly unable to walk another step, I would find myself calling home to see if anyone in my family wanted to go with me to the local 24-hour pancake house. This was far from my regular diet—you won't believe what sorts of strange things you'll crave at the end of a day of catering! As I dug into three pancakes, eggs-over-easy, and a cup of coffee, I'd slowly begin to unwind. After the meal, I'd go home and fall easily into bed, my last conscious thoughts being that I earned the upcoming good night's rest—and then some!

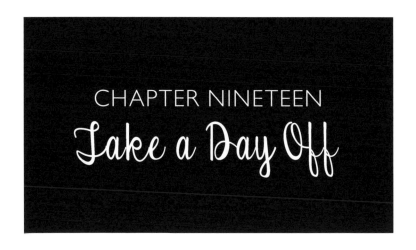

CHAPTER NINETEEN
Take a Day Off

THAT'S ALL THERE IS TO IT.

CHAPTER TWENTY
What Comes Next?

AFTER YOU HAVE RESTED AND CATERED TO YOUR
OWN NEEDS, YOU'LL INEVITABLY ASK YOURSELF:
"DO I EVER WANT TO DO THIS AGAIN?"

. . . .

My answer to the above question is a resounding YES!—*after* I've had a good 24 hours to recharge. Indeed, it is a crazy business, and yet I truly love it. That love generates the motivation and energy I need to do it all again, job after job. If you feel similarly, then you have chosen the right profession. With your first job complete, you are truly on your way to a blooming business.

But wait a minute! Before you embrace the next client, you must finish up with the first. Strategically, it is wise to give your client the bill while her enthusiasm and excitement is still palpable. While some companies provide their client with the final bill *at* the event, there are two reasons why I don't. One, the night of the event should be a pure celebration, unmarred by financial matters. And two, there is usually some "settling up" to do *after* the completion of the job, which makes it impractical to finalize the bill beforehand. You may be waiting for the rental company to mail you a new statement. The liquor company may not have credited you for the unopened bottles. You may need to recalculate your final staff hours. As soon as you are able to pull these numbers together, get out the bill, whether via snail mail, email, or delivery.

Let me share my favorite method of bill delivery. I like to drop the invoice at the client's home, along with a small gift and a Thank You note. I make sure that the note communicates that I genuinely enjoyed working with the client and that I appreciate their business. This is a warm, personal way to request payment. As for gifts, I make sure that they reflect the style of Miss Jeanies. Small, tasteful options include hand towels, teas, gourmet treats, coffee cups, and homemade cookies or jams make wonderful choices. I always prepare these in advance so that I will have them ready ASAP.

These little packages can be made even more special with the addition of one more element: a few photos from the event. Party-givers usually have so many demands on their attention that they don't really take it all in, and photographs are a terrific way for them to see what they missed. And of course, snapshots of your beautiful food presentation are a great marketing tool. Think about putting some of the best photos in an inexpensive photo holder and adding that to your gift. If you're not hand-delivering a gift along with your bill, you can still include photos with bills sent via e-mail or US mail. And even if you don't plan to send this client any photos, use your camera or your cell phone to capture images of the event. These can be used to promote your business in the future.

History in the Making

Along with a book of our menus and a collection of Thank Yous we've received over the years, one thing I've never put together is an "album" depicting Miss Jeanies' history. Do not make the same mistake as I did. No matter how busy you are, stop for a second to snap some photos. Alternatively, if there's a photographer who's working the event, you can obtain photos from him or her. You may be able to get their photos free or at reduced cost by offering to refer clients their way or otherwise bartering your services.

You can get in the habit of documenting your business before you have your first job. What seem like inconsequential moments may ultimately be turning points in the story of your business. So take a picture when you make a centerpiece out of edible items, even if no one sees it but you. Write down the story of how your Grandma's recipe inspired your seasonings. Detail how you cleverly packaged Christmas gifts for your friends.

You just don't know where this is all going, I promise its going somewhere.

Feedback and Disappointments

It usually doesn't take long before I hear back from a client with comments, either positive or negative. Thank goodness, they're usually more positive than negative. But still, I wait by the phone like a teenager waiting to hear from a crush. It's amazing how vulnerable and excited I feel as I wait to learn what the client thought of the event.

Despite my eagerness (and impatience), I don't bug clients who don't get in touch right away. They're likely trying to get back in the swing of things, all while facing exhaustion, lingering visitors, and a phone that's ringing off the hook.

Some companies actively solicit feedback, although mine does not. There are pros and cons to this practice. Some clients may be uncomfortable in terms of the etiquette of criticizing their caterer. If they do have a grievance, they prefer to let it go, rather than embarrass the provider. No matter how much you communicate that you appreciate *any and all* feedback, and that you'll do your best to make retribution, these clients be hesitant to confront you. Other clients feel no discomfort when providing negative feedback. They appreciate having a sounding board and they'll put it to good use in hopes of hearing you apologize.

Wait for it to ring? Or pick it up and dial? It's your call.

Regardless of whether negative feedback is solicited or not, when it does come, there are two things that need to be done:

1) Attempt to remedy the situation

2) Take steps to prevent the situation from reoccurring

Let's begin with remedying the situation. Even the most careful, most experienced caterers occasionally find themselves needing to do a bit of damage control. Perhaps the risotto was too gooey, or a staff member spilled a glass of water on a table. **It is inevitable that there will be small disappointments, as no job is perfect.** The good news is that many common disappointments can be prevented with a bit of forethought, and those that cannot be prevented can be remedied skillfully. What follows are some common disappointments and suggested solutions:

The Problem: "I didn't get to try the Indonesian chicken sauté."
The Solution: This is easy to prevent by putting aside a sample of each appetizer for the host and hostess ahead of time.

The Problem: "I was hoping there would be enough leftovers for my family's dinner tomorrow."
The Solution: This too can be prevented. Before the start of the party, review your leftover policy a second time with the client. If you have guaranteed her enough leftovers to feed 4 the next day, make sure she gets them as promised. And clarify that you guaranteed enough for 4, not 8, not 10. If food runs low during the party, you should dip into what you had set aside: your first priority is always feeding the guests at the event.

The Problem: "There wasn't enough salmon on the buffet for everyone. I had to eat the beef entree instead."
The Solution: Explain to the client that while you had anticipated that people would be equally interested in the two main courses, ultimately so many guests chose salmon that it ran low. And if you really want to make amends, cook another salmon and take it to her.

The Problem: "I was in line at the buffet when you ran out of main course plates. I couldn't get my food until someone went to find more."
The Solution: That's bad timing for you. Apologize, but still send the bill without making adjustments.

The Problem: "The cloth napkins were a slightly different shade of white than the tablecloths."
The Solution: Assuming that you're unable to get the linens replaced before the start of the party, make do with what you've been given, but ask the rental company to reduce your bill. Send the client her bill without adjusting the charges, but let her know that should the rental company refund part of your money later on, you will pass on the funds to her.

Now, onto preventing mistakes from reoccurring. When you or your staff make a once-in-a-lifetime mistake, you cannot do anything besides admit to it, apologize, and move on. But when a mistake happens more than once, or you receive criticism regarding something inherent to the way your company does things, you have the opportunity to change. To make use of this opportunity, you need to thoroughly look at the issue, figure out what's causing it, and then come up with potential solutions.

I don't rely on client feedback exclusively to learn about deep-rooted issues with my company, as it's rare that something significant can go wrong, especially more than once, without my being aware of it. If I don't pick up on an error, my staff usually does. In order to put this awareness to use, our core staff routinely meets to review what happened at an event and what's generally happening in the milieu of our company. We aim to come up with solutions. This is the best way to better ourselves and the company. Reflection and introspection are key to setting future goals and expectations. **There is always room for improvement, and by reexamining and reevaluating your jobs, you will see your business develop even further.**

A Disputed Bill

The preceding examples, such as the salmon shortage or the mismatched linens, are what I would deem *disappointments* with the event itself. A grievance regarding the *cost* of the event is another matter. A disputed bill is one of the most discouraging, energy-sucking things that can befall a caterer. All the passion, consideration, and hard work you put in, and this is what you get? What to do?

Even if you *know* that you're in the right, you must listen attentively to a client's grievance. Many squabbles can be laid to rest as soon as you show the client the relevant accounting information, be it a breakdown of staff charges, a rental invoice, a beverage receipt, etc. (This is where organization will reap its rewards, or where your disorganization may come back to haunt you). There's a limit, however, to how much detail you should give the client. **Your actual food and cooking costs do not need to be justified.** If you charged $30 per person for food, you have no obligation to show your client the grocery bill for the chicken breasts or tell her how many hours of labor went into cooking the Chicken Marsala. That's your private information. It is not up to your client to judge whether it took too long for you to cook or whether you should have bought a cheaper brand of meat.

If the records that a client requests reveal that I went over budget, a little explaining becomes necessary. If I've charged more for staff than originally estimated, I explain that the party went a little longer than anticipated. If I bought ten extra bottles of juice, I explain that we ran low in the midst of the party and went to the store for emergency replenishments. Once a client knows the reason for the discrepancy between budget and estimate, she is usually okay with the final numbers.

So do I ever adjust a bill? Depending on the client, I will on occasion adjust a charge a tiny bit, just to demonstrate flexibility and good spirit. If I can take $100 off a bill to pacify my client, it may be worth it in terms of the time and energy saved by avoiding a drawn-out argument. I may be upset over the lost money, but the client maintains a good feeling about my company and about what she paid for her event, and that's what matters most.

WHAT'S NEXT?

So you've moved beyond your first job. What to do if the phone is not ringing? The days are passing. You're desperate to get your hands on another job, but there are no nibbles. What can you do? **Do one thing a day to promote your business.** Chat with someone at your day job about the business your have launched. Listen to a TED talk or watch a YouTube video on email marketing. Put a catchy flyer up at your health club. Bring attention to your company. And when things seem bleak, remind yourself that just because you haven't received an inquiry does not mean that your outreach efforts have fallen on deaf ears. Somewhere, unbeknownst to you, a guest who attended your event is singing your praises to a co-worker. The guest passes the co-worker one of your business cards. The co-worker may not call you for a month, or for three. But sooner or later, an opportunity will come your way.

Regardless of when the second job comes your way, you will re-peat many of the steps we've walked through in these chapters. This time around, you'll be a little more confident. Some things may start to feel like second nature. Yes, you'll still second-guess yourself at times. You may feel like you're still a novice at preparing a budget, or that your skill at estimating food quantities is coming along frustratingly slow. Yet, think of all that you've learned to do. You started with an idea, an inkling that you could do something with food. You weren't sure it was realistic, yet you pushed past your doubts and listened to those who encouraged you. You named your company and started marketing. When someone showed interest in your product, you cre-ated a menu and priced it, gave them a proposal, and got hired!

Perhaps your confidence faltered here; you wondered, "Now how do I pull this off?" But in the following weeks or months, you moved ahead. You made sure your kitchen was functional and prop-erly-equipped. You faced a flood of information regarding food safety, but instead of being paralyzed by the amount of responsibility upon you, you persevered. You organized your shopping excursions, figured out the quantities you needed, and got it all ready to cook. And maybe once you started cooking you found yourself getting into a flow: work-ing with food, after all, was what you wanted to do in the first place.

Then came the day of the event, and a bevy of new worries. Yet even if you had wanted to, you could not have turned back, for the momentum of the party grabbed hold of you. And before you knew it, the guests were there, the food was served, and everything came together. You felt an unbelievable mix of excitement, pride and shock: you had done it.

So maybe you didn't do it perfectly. But by now, you have probably ascertained that I am not a perfectionist, nor do I believe in perfection. There is actually a beauty in not being perfect. The beauty is in the art of knowing what to do in situations that are not exactly what you envisioned. It's when the going gets tough that a caterer can truly prove herself. Being able to problem-solve, to troubleshoot, to improvise, and to think on one's feet are fundamental assets of a food entrepreneur.

If at any time you doubt that you're on the right track with this work, just think: Are you still waking up early with thoughts of your menu? Does your mind turn to visions of an event when you're supposed to be focused on something else? If so, you've got it. You'll be fine. Ultimately, all your extraordinary hard work will be worth it.

If this book has excited you, I am certain that a career in food, whichever niche you choose, is for you. Be patient and keep moving: you will be at this until you are ninety-two. I certainly plan to.

All best, Miss Jeanie

POSTSCRIPT

What if you know you adore baking your mother's brown sugar cookies, yet now that you've read this book and thought long and hard about it, you're not sure you like the thought of catering. Loading and unloading a van during snowstorms. Having to get to the fish market at dawn. Dealing with a hundred strangers at every event. Great news! Much of what you have learnt in this book is applicable to other parts of the food business. You can use the information contained herein to make *your* ideas into a food business.

YOU CAN MAKE FOOD WORK

Fresh Fruits and Veggies

Though it may sound simple, it's really hard to figure out how far ahead you can prep a green salad and prep your greens. I am insistent on having our greens be as crisp and unwilted as possible so that our salads taste as if we just made them seconds before. This salad recipe is one of my all time favorites. You can modify it according to the menu you are creating.

Tropical Greens with Thai Mint Vinagrette

INGREDIENTS FOR DRESSING:
1 clove garlic, very finely minced
2 Tbsp ¼ finely minced ginger
¼ cup safflower oil
1 teaspoon Asian chili sauce
2 tablespoons thin soy sauce
2 tablespoons light brown sugar
1 teaspoon grated lime zest
2 Tbsp freshly squeezed lime juice
1 teaspoon grated orange zest
¼ cup orange juice
¼ teaspoon salt

INGREDIENTS FOR SALAD:
artisan greens
Berries
Mango or Papayas
1 or 2 avocados
Macadamia Nuts for toasting
fresh mint
fresh cilantro

Make dressing 2-3 days ahead of time by pulsing ingredients in a food processor. Retaste it day of party. May want to readjust to taste

Nuts can be toasted several days ahead of time. After toasting, let them cool down well. Store it a tin or plastic container with tight lid.

Wash greens and berries (separately) a day ahead of time. Pat very dry and place between pieces of paper towels. Cover well with plastic wrap and refrigerate.

If using a mango or papaya, peel it a day ahead of time. Scoop out seeds and cover very tightly with plastic wrap. Put melon in plastic bags in the refrigerator.

Assemble greens, berries, melon, nuts, and herbs at the job. Place in refrigerator until 10 or so minutes before serving. At the last minute, cut avocados (I do not suggest cutting them ahead of time). Dress salad and serve ASAP.

Acknowledgements

"Just put it down on paper, and I'll help you pull it together." Kayla Small put in endless hours deciphering her way through my illegible handwriting and my out-of-place paragraphs. An amazing copy writer and designer, Kayla has taken this book from paper to publication.

Of course, this book would not have come into being without the business success story behind it: Miss Jeanies Catering Company, twenty years old and stronger than ever. It goes without saying that my staff were integral to that success. But what's less obvious is the contribution of my two sons, Ben and Jake. For years, they put up with a garlic-drenched mother breathlessly running in to watch the second half of their basketball games. They learned not to climb into the backseat of our van without checking the seats for spills of Sherried Mushroom Soup or Thai Mint Vinaigrette. And they never fail to let me know that they're proud of and happy for me. Thank you.

My husband, Jay, was my first boyfriend and is the best friend any one could ask for. Whether the adventure was changing careers, opening a take-out restaurant, or writing this book, he supported me steadily throughout. His continuing encouragement that my catering story was one worth sharing has made this book possible. Jay has listened, learned to make dinner, and spent many Saturdays alone. I am eternally grateful for his selflessness, and for his love.

20978930R00142

Made in the USA
Middletown, DE
15 June 2015